WONDERS
OF THE
WORLD

Created by olo.éditions
www.oloeditions.com
115, rue d'Aboukir
75002 Paris
France

EDITORIAL CONCEPTION
Nicolas Marçais

ART DIRECTION
Philippe Marchand

EDITORIAL
Diane Routex

AUTHOR
Christopher Westhorp

PROOFREADER
Joanna Chisholm

Cover credits: (front cover) © Robbie Fair/Getty;
(back cover) © Sylvain Sonnet/Corbis, © Jason Hawkes/Corbis,
© Richard Roscoe/Stocktrek Images/Corbis.

ISBN: 978-2-9532483-9-5

Date of printing: August 2013
Printed in Asia

WONDERS OF THE WORLD

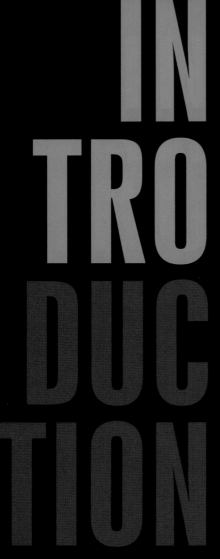

INTRODUCTION

From magical paintings made on the walls of a European cave complex during the Stone Age to glass-and-steel skyscrapers erected in the desert of Arabia in the twenty-first century, *Wonders of the World* features nearly 90 diverse places across six continents, which capture the best of human inventiveness and accomplishment.

It is, of course, nigh on impossible for a single, readable, volume to capture the best of architectural creativity. This magnificently illustrated book is global in scope and represents a wide variety of types, in form, materials, and the mix of motivations, whether political, religious, military, or commercial. Vernacular houses and luxurious palaces, temples and mosques, gardens and necropolises, castles and city squares, remote retreats and planned urban grids, bridges and titanic statues—all appear within.

Many structures are manifestations of humankind's profound need to connect to the sacred and provide a forum and focus for worship. Other choices express secular abstract notions, such as the universal desire for liberty, while a few places owe their existence to egotism and the need to impress rather than anything more profound or practical. There are sites where the designers and workers will always remain unknown to us, while others we know were shaped by the genius of individuals, such as Leonardi da Vinci and Michelangelo.

The selection includes mysterious megalithic monuments at Stonehenge and Carnac; memorials for eternity, erected to honor divine rulers, at Giza and Abu Simbel; triumphs of hydrology at Petra and M'zab; engineering marvels that have become famous worldwide, such as the Eiffel Tower and the Golden Gate Bridge; national icons, such as the Sydney Opera House and Mount Rushmore; and citadels, fortified towns, and castles, including Granada's

Alhambra, Essaouira's ramparts, and Bavaria's Neuschwanstein, which influenced Walt Disney. The results of all this incredible human endeavor, boundless imagination, and skill can be humbling, uplifting and awe-inspiring—a sense of wonder familiar to anyone who has visited an acclaimed tourist attraction or a famous city.

Some sites speak to us powerfully through the ages. We can imagine the terror that the doomed people at Pompeii might have endured; we can experience delight at the beautiful sights within Córdoba's La Mezquita; and we can sympathize with the grieving husband whose mausolueum for his beloved wife is Agra's Taj Mahal.

Alongside these are such global symbols of world heritage as the Athenian Acropolis, St. Peter's Basilica in Rome, and the Forbidden City in China, which means that what follows is a journey through some of the finest treasures of civilization.

TEMPLE OF RAMESSES II
ABU SIMBEL, EGYPT

A tribute to his divine self by the great warrior-king who had it built during his 67-year reign (*c.*1279–*c.*1213BCE), the east-facing temple at Abu Simbel cuts into the rock face, as if declaring an intention to last for eternity.

Dedicated to Ramesses II and the gods Re-Harakhte, Amun-Re, and Ptah, the temple was completed in the 1250s BCE in what was the Nubia frontierland—a statement of the pharaoh's power and confidence. The entrance is an Egyptian pylon, or gateway structure, flanked by two pairs of seated statues of Ramesses II, each 66 feet high. Inside is a main hall that is nearly 30 feet high, its roof held up by pillars in the form of massive statues of the king as Osiris, lord of the afterlife, with rooms beyond that lead ultimately to a shrine. Ramesses II built more monuments than any other pharaoh, and, as with many of his buildings, the temple incorporates accounts of the events of his reign, including his great military victories against his enemies.

In the 1960s, in an impressive feat of engineering, the temple—along with those of Nefertari (his principal wife) and Philae—was dismantled and rebuilt on higher ground to prevent it being lost under the waters of Lake Nasser, which was created by the construction of the Aswan High Dam.

MACHU PICCHU
CUZCO, PERU

In July 1911 American explorer Hiram Bingham stumbled across what he believed was Vilcabamba, the last seat of Inca resistance to the Spanish. In fact, he had found a royal estate that is famous today as a symbol of Inca civilization.

Built for Pachacuti in about 1450 at an altitude of 8,000 feet above a gorge of the Urubamba River, this towering citadel sits on a ridge between two peaks known as Huayna Picchu ("Young Picchu") and Machu Picchu ("Old Picchu"). The typically Incan mortar-less stone structures include residences for royals and retainers, temples, baths, plazas, platforms, and agricultural terraces. Although the town's remoteness may have protected its small population in the wake of the conquest of the Inca Empire, the real motive for constructing the complex is unknown—it may simply have been an elite retreat from congested Cuzco. The key, however, may lie in cosmology and sacred geography. In Andean culture, a place such as this was called a *huaca*—a part of the landscape that possessed great sacred power. The town seems to have been laid out with a religious quarter, and more than half of the buildings appear to have had a ceremonial purpose. An older theory is that Machu Picchu was a sanctuary for the Acclas ("Chosen Women"), female followers of Inti, the sun god.

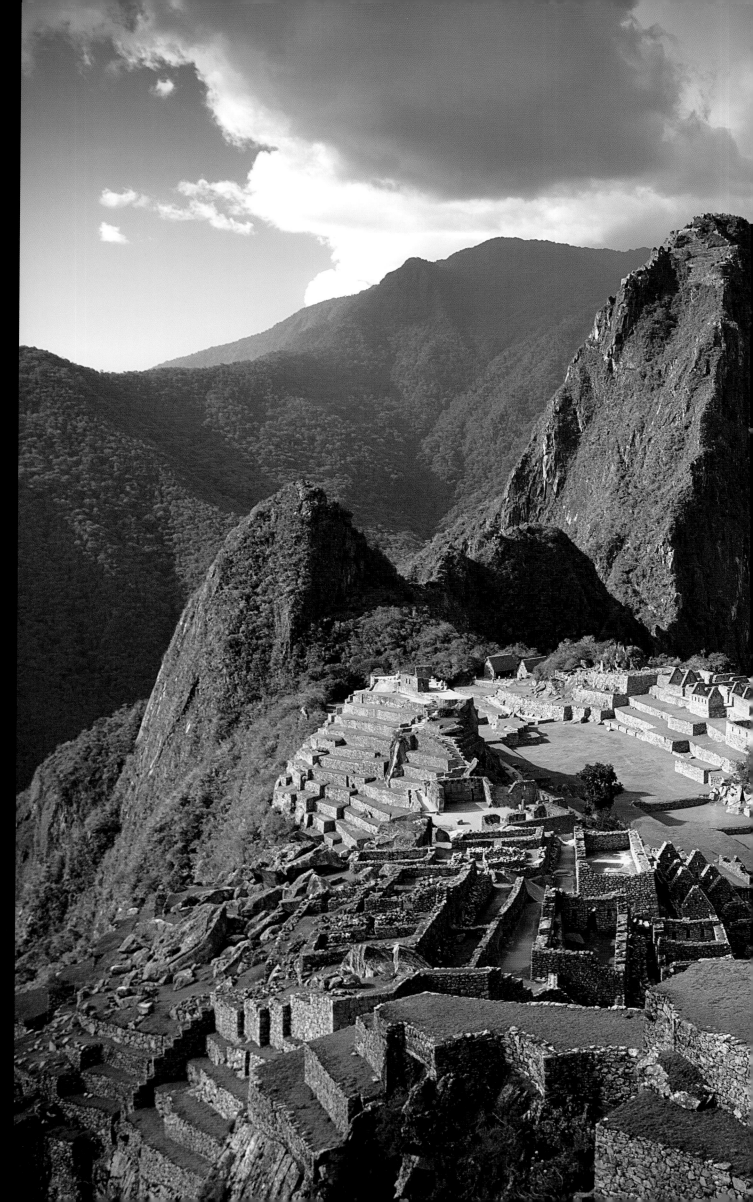

ANGKOR WAT
ANGKOR, CAMBODIA

This twelfth-century masterpiece of Khmer architecture is a sacred microcosm, a "temple mountain" whose five central towers symbolize Mount Meru, which in Indian mythology is the axis of the world and home of the gods at the center of the universe.

The vast religious complex at Angkor, the capital city of the Indianized Khmer empire, was decreed by King Suryavarman II in about 1113 as his dynastic temple and mortuary shrine. (A theory supported by the fact that the counterclockwise direction of some of the bas-reliefs are in accordance with the order of Brahmanic funeral rites.). He dedicated it to the royal cult of Vishnu. In extent and splendor the temple is comparable to any of the largest sacred structures in South India—a pilgrim wishing to circumambulate would need to walk several miles. The advancing jungle that surrounds the site can mean that trees take root and cause damage (following pages). However, since its decline began in the 1400s, the temple has been afforded some protection by virtue of its moat or ritual purification pool, which represents the waters surrounding the world. Angkor was popularized in the West in the 1860s through the posthumously published writings of French naturalist Henri Mouhot, who declared it grander than anything left by Greece or Rome.

PAGAN
MANDALAY, BURMA

In the past 1,500 years kingdoms have risen and fallen beside the Irrawaddy River in what is now Burma (Myanmar). The evidence of a great civilization is apparent to anyone who visits Pagan, an astonishing city of golden shrines.

The Myanma people founded their capital of Pagan, or Bagan, in 849CE and by the reign of King Anawrahta (1044–1077), the city had attained supremacy in Burma. This lasted until 1257, when the Mongols overran Pagan.

Buddhism had taken root in the region earlier among the Mon people, and it was a Mon monk who converted Anawrahta, which led to Therevada Buddhism dominating the kingdom. State patronage then played a major role in the development of monuments at Pagan and elsewhere, many bearing both Indian and Mon stylistic influences.

It is a tradition in Burma that to found a new temple is more meritorious than to maintain an old one, which may explain why Burma has more temples and bell-shaped pagodas (known as *zedi* or *paya* rather than *stupa*) than anywhere else in the Buddhist world. At Pagan alone, within an area of about 25 square miles, there are more than 900 temples, 500 *zedi*, and 400 monasteries, as well as the remains of countless more, hence its former nickname "city of four million pagodas."

CITY OF PETRA
PETRA, JORDAN

Forgotten for centuries, this city hewn out of stone—Petra is from the Latin *petrae* ("rock")—still resonates with the mysteries of its great past as the capital of the Nabatean people.

Few discoveries can be more thrilling than to trek across the desert of southern Jordan, venture for nearly a mile along a dim and narrow gorge known as the Siq, and emerge into sunlight and the magnificent façade of Al Khazneh el Faroun—the so-called Treasury of the Pharaoh (following pages), although its actual function in ancient times is unknown.

Petra was once a hydrological marvel of man-made water channels and cisterns, which supported a population of about 30,000 scattered across 400 square miles. This natural fortress of a city developed from about 600BCE onward, growing prosperous from the frankincense caravan trade thanks to its strategic location at the crossroads between Arabia, Egypt, Palestine, and Syria.

Petra's peak was brief (*c.*150BCE–*c.*150CE), then it was annexed by Rome and the trade rerouted. Some of the city's wealth was spent on temples, theaters, and tombs, many of which remain obscured by rubble and drifting sand. Majestically set in this monumental landscape is El Deir ("the Monastery"), a remarkable cave church with an imposing frontage that conceals a large chamber for worship.

THE COLOSSEUM
ROME, ITALY

This one-time pleasure palace for the Roman people is best known today as the imperial arena where gladiators fought to the death.

Built in 70–82CE, the Flavian Amphitheater, as it was originally known, was the first permanent example of its kind to be built in Rome. Vespasian (reigned 69–79) initiated the project but it was his son Titus who inaugurated it in 80, with 100 days of festivities dedicated to killing as entertainment. The name by which we know the structure today derives from a gigantic (100-feet-plus) bronze statue that once stood near here, a legacy from Nero's extravagant villa, the Domus Aurea.

The stadium was elliptical in plan and nearly 160 feet tall, with a system of interconnecting concentric corridors beneath the converging ramps of seats on four floors. These were segregated by social class, with senators nearest and women and plebians furthest away. A crowd of 50,000-plus was able to come in, and later leave, quickly and efficiently through 76 entrances. Additionally, the emperor and his family had their own entrance, as did the gladiators and musicians, and the authorities such as priests and vestal virgins.

Still in use until the 520s, the Colosseum is consecrated because of the Christian martyrs who died within, and every Good Friday the pope celebrates a Via Crucis ceremony there.

ROUSSANOU MONASTERY
METEORA, GREECE

Gripping a mountainous pinnacle a thousand feet above the ground, this monastery at Meteora (which in Greek means "suspended in the air") in Thessaly, northern Greece, has been home to a religious community since the 1540s.

Inspired by the ideal of simple living to demonstrate commitment to Christ, from the eleventh century onward 24 spectacularly located monasteries were built in this vicinity, mostly in the fourteenth and fifteenth centuries. Monks used scaffolds to ascend the rocks in order to insert joists into the stone, then rope ladders, baskets, and nets were used to move people and materials. The monastic inhabitants followed in the wake of Christian hermits who had taken refuge among these so-called "heavenly columns" in the ninth century, the first of whom is believed to have been Barnabas. Stone ladders were not carved until the twentieth century.

Although this way of life is today threatened with extinction, Roussanou is one of six monasteries that are still inhabited by those pledged to lives of prayer and work. Dedicated to St. Barbara and occupied by nuns, it is known for its sixteenth-century Byzantine frescoes in the Church of the Transfiguration of Christ. Two other deserted Meteora monasteries have been restored and opened to tourism.

AYUTTHAYA HISTORICAL PARK
AYUTTHAYA, THAILAND

During Thailand's Khmer period, immigrants from southern China established a succession of powerful kingdoms, including Sukhothai in the north (c.1240) and Ayudhya, or Ayutthaya, in the south (1351), which was to absorb Sukhothai.

For more than 400 years the city of Ayutthaya, an island at the confluence of three rivers, was the capital. French visitors reported that the capital of what they called "Siam" was the most beautiful city in the East and rivaled Paris. Today, Ayutthaya is a graveyard of temples. Centuries of destruction and looting mean the ruins can only hint at the city's former magnificence—in 1895 the governor even had the walls pulled down to make the foundations for a ring road.

Just an hour's drive to the north of Bangkok, Ayutthaya even in a decayed condition is still a big tourist attraction. Khmer influence is noticeable in the central tower, or *prang*, surrounded by smaller ones. There are also statues of the seated Buddha making his earth-touching gesture. Many of the statues have characteristic elongated ears and a royal crown.

The historical park was created in the 1970s and the site was awarded World Heritage status in 1991—an event celebrated each year with a festival featuring fireworks and pageants at one of the historical *wats*.

HAGIA SOPHIA
ISTANBUL, TURKEY

This tremendous space is the acme of Byzantine architecture, as intended by its sponsor Emperor Justinian, who wanted a new cathedral for Constantinople of unsurpassed plan, size, permanence, and decorative richness.

Hagia Sophia, dedicated to "divine wisdom," was built in just five years (532–537). A mystical circular form was emphasized through an ambitious new enclosure of space that accentuated the dome, its weight dispersed by smaller domes around it, which created a huge central space free of columns. Sunlight through the 40 windows at the top helped the mosaics to glisten and made the dome appear to float in the heavens.

To symbolize the dominance of Christianity over paganism, Justinian used pillars and arches from temples at Baalbeck and Ephesus. He also put on prominent display such elements as a stone medallion of Medusa (removed to a museum in 1871), which was understood to avert evil influence—a cultural belief in the "evil eye" can still be found in Turkey.

After the conquest of Constantinople in 1453, it was the Turks' turn for triumphalism and the church became a mosque, with buttresses and minarets added. In 1934 it was secularized into a museum, with Islamic medallions (following pages) still hanging inside.

RAPA NUI NATIONAL PARK
EASTER ISLAND, CHILE

The silent stone sentinels of this enigmatic island, more than 2,000 miles from the mainland, have witnessed humankind's ingenuity as well as its environmental idiocy.

Rapa Nui (formerly Easter Island) is home to some 2,000 Rapanui, whose Polynesian ancestors probably settled in the eighth century CE and went on to erect the island's distinctive stone figures of deified ancestors, known as *moai*. In the 1600s it is believed that competition for resources produced two warring polities, and in the upheaval that ensued most of the weighty *moai* were toppled. Today, nearly 900 still survive.

These fifteen *moai* occupy a ceremonial platform, or *ahu*, at Tongariki in the east of the island, and were restored in the 1960s. Dozens of similar *ahu* are set into hills and around the coastline.

How were these heavy figures ever moved around? Island oral tradition says that the statues "walked," animated by ancestral force, or *mana*. The old tale may well contain some truth because experiments show that groups of people can use ropes to coax a *moai* along by rocking it gently.

After years of cultural and economic neglect, in 2011 the indigenous clans of the world's most remote inhabited island proclaimed a king and began to seek sovereignty and Easter Island's independence from Chile.

ALHAMBRA
GRANADA, SPAIN

Set on a rocky outcrop, surrounded by woodland and majestically framed by the snow-capped Sierra Nevada, the palace and fortress complex of the Alhambra fulfills the Islamic theme of earthly paradise.

After the collapse of the caliphate of Córdoba in the 1030s, Al-Andalus was engulfed by civil wars. In the 1230s Muhammad ibn Yusuf ben Nasr established the Nasrid kingdom in Granada. There he fortified this ancient citadel site as the residence of his court (Madinat al-Hamra—"the red city"), where several Nasrid palaces and many houses of high-ranking officials were built, alongside the military barracks, or Alcazaba, of the royal guard.

In 1492 the city became the last Muslim-held site to fall to the Catholic Monarchs during the reconquest of the peninsula, and in 1527 the Charles V Palace was added. Adjoining the Alhambra's monuments on the hilltop are the magnificent gardens of the Generalife, where the Nasrid emirs once relaxed.

Over the centuries the site fell into disrepair until it was "rediscovered" by travelers in the nineteenth century, including its great restoration champion, American writer Washington Irving. As a byword for luxury, Alhambra then became a popular name for movie theaters. This UNESCO World Heritage Site is now one of Spain's leading historical attractions.

Built in stone for eternity, the Great Pyramid is a spectacular funerary work—the heart of Giza's royal necropolis, one of the marvels of the ancient world, and Egypt's most enduring symbol.

Perfectly proportioned, the pyramids at Giza were built some 4,500 years ago and were once encased in dazzling white Tura limestone, with perhaps a cap of gold. Buried there are three pharaohs of the fourth dynasty: Menkaure (left, with three subsidiary pyramids), Khafre (center), and, in the Great Pyramid (right), Khufu (reigned 2585–2560BCE).

The pyramid expresses three key things about ancient Egyptian culture: the power of the king, the cult of the dead, and the importance of the sun god.

Khufu's pyramid, which Herodotus says took 30 years to build, is thought to contain 92 million cubic feet of stone—more than two million limestone blocks, each weighing a couple of tons.

Oriented to true north, the Great Pyramid has a base that is 756 feet square and originally had a height of 481 feet. It contains three chambers on different levels, reached by sloping galleries. From the red granite-lined chamber in which Khufu was buried, two square tunnels, each 8 inches wide, run all the way to the outside of the pyramid—perhaps the means by which the king's spirit could ascend on a celestial ramp to the heavens.

BOROBUDUR
JAVA, INDONESIA

Nothing in Southeast Asia rivals the form and mass of Borobodur, built by the Sailendra kings of central Java in the early ninth century CE.

Borobudur is a three-dimensional meditational device—a cosmic *mandala* in stone. Its combination of the circle, representing the celestial realm, and the square, representing the material world of the Earth, means that the structure of the temple reproduces the hidden one of the universe. A staircase on each side of the square base enables devotees to ascend through the circular levels (following pages) to the top—thereby making a journey from the earthly world to the summit of the cosmic axis, the realm of inner vision and the ultimate insight of the Buddha on Mount Meru.

Adorning the terraces are thousands of reliefs (some now obscured) depicting *karma* and decorative panels with scenes from Buddhist texts. The upper level has 72 lattice stonework *stupa*s, arranged in decreasing circles of 32, 24, and 16 around the dome at the top. The *stupa*s contain statues of the Buddha in meditation, carved out of volcanic andesite.

After only a century this site was abandoned when power on the island shifted eastwards, possibly due to an eruption. Undergrowth and volcanic ash had obscured it when it was rediscovered in 1814 by Stamford Raffles, who initiated its restoration.

M'ZAB VALLEY
HARDAÏA, ALGERIA

Although it bears some similarities to the Berber fortified architecture of Morocco, M'zab is a culturally distinctive valley oasis some 400 miles south of Algiers.

This area was settled about 1,000 years ago by a branch of the Zenata Berber people who had become Ibadites, a minority form of Islam. The land and the living space were organized in accordance with their beliefs.

The agriculture on the valley floor is fed by ingenious hydrological systems. On higher ground are five walled *ksar*, or fortified villages: Beni Isguen, Bou Noura, El Atteuf, Ghardaïa, and Melika. The division of each *ksar* into neighborhoods reflected the pattern of irrigated land ownership. Each *ksar* has a mosque, school, market, and a network of streets: wide ones to connect the community facilities and narrow alleyways to the houses, laid out in concentric circles.

The simple, functional architecture, has curving walls but it lacks color and ornamentation. The houses have defined female and male areas, and were built around courtyards: an enclosed one on the ground floor, a more open one on the upper floor, and a partitioned roof terrace that could be used for open-air sleeping. The culture has been weakened in the modern era, but the environmentally adapted architecture of the M'zab has made it a region of interest to urban planners.

ST. PETER'S BASILICA
VATICAN CITY

Emperor Constantine built the original church here on the site of the martyred first bishop of Rome. In 1506–1626 the rebuilt St. Peter's became the magnificent heart of Christendom.

This domed basilica—so huge that St. Paul's in London would fit inside—was shaped by people ranging from Bramante to Michelangelo. Outside, statues symbolize the transformative power of faith: the balustrade of the neoclassical façade has 13 statues—each nearly 20 feet high—of Christ the Redeemer, St. John the Baptist, and 11 apostles. In keeping with the Baroque idea of a drama involving the faithful, more than 100,000 people can gather in the piazza (1656–1667, by Bernini) before the central window where the pope gives his blessing at Christmas and Easter. The colonnades, crowned by 140 statues of saints, were conceived as welcoming arms that embrace the piazza. Inside, beneath the dome and at the heart of the basilica, is the Altar of the Confessio. Beneath the altar is St. Peter's tomb. The altar is surmounted by a masterful bronze-gilt *baldacchino*, or canopy, on huge, twisted columns. Inlaid in the mosaic around the dome's base (following pages) are the words with which Jesus gave Peter (*petrus* means "rock") the authority to establish the Church: "You are Peter and on this rock I will build my church…" (from Matthew 16:18–19).

STONEHENGE
WILTSHIRE, ENGLAND

This world-famous circle of stones near Salisbury shows the creative genius of Neolithic man. Dominating the landscape for millennia, its size and precision assembly make it a worthy object of awe.

The oldest parts of the megalithic monument are the outer bank and ditch henge, dating from *c.*3000BCE. The stones were erected about a millennium later. Resembling a vast open-air temple or a ritual enclosure, the site may well be the focus of a larger monument complex in the area, which includes many burial mounds. However, there is also persuasive evidence of celestial associations: an opening to the northwest appears to align with the moon at midwinter, while at the northeast an avenue from the center aligns to the midsummer sunrise. Thus at dawn on the summer solstice an observer in the center of Stonehenge will witness the sun rise over the "heel" stone, which is situated beyond the ditch.

Arguably the most remarkable aspect of Stonehenge is its construction, with huge lintels continuously capping the 30-stone outer circle and also used to make five inner trilithons, locked with carefully shaped joints. Wiltshire sandstone sarsens are combined with Pembroke bluestone, quarried far away in the Preseli mountains of west Wales and believed to have had healing powers.

POTALA PALACE
LHASA, TIBET, CHINA

Towering imposingly over Lhasa from the slopes of Mount Marpori, this building was named after Mount Potalaka, the celestial abode of Avalokiteshvara, the *bodhisattva* of compassion and the patron deity of Tibet.

Tibetans believe their country has had two emanations of Avalokiteshvara: King Songsten Gampo and the "Great Fifth"—the Dalai Lama of the Gelugpa religious order for whom this palace was built between 1642 and 1650 on the site of Gampo's seventh-century palace, which was destroyed by lightning. As the sacred leader of a now theocratic state, the Dalai Lama wanted the palace to be a residence, a monastery, a seat of government, a fortress, and a powerful national symbol.

It is in fairly typical Tibetan style, with sloping walls and flat roofs, albeit in an elaborate form with much gilding and many areas exquisitely decorated with religious iconography within its 1,000 rooms. The palace has two sections: the White Palace, where government was conducted and foreign envoys received, and the Red Palace, containing temples and shrines, including the reliquary tombs of eight Dalai Lamas. Until the era of modern skyscrapers, the 13-story edifice was one of the tallest in the world at nearly 390 feet high.

CARTHAGE
TUNIS, TUNISIA

In what is now a fashionable suburb of Tunis, archaeologists are revealing Roman and Punic Carthage, North Africa's most important ancient metropolis.

Established in the ninth century BCE as a trading entrepôt on the Gulf of Tunis by Phoenicians from Tyre, this city became the center of a seaborne commercial empire that dominated the region. In 146BCE, after losing the Punic Wars to Rome, Carthage was demolished and plowed over, until in 49BCE Julius Caesar initiated a new one over the ruins. The city was later an important regional center of Christianity and capital of the Byzantine province of Africa, until destroyed again during the Arab conquest of the 690s.

Perhaps no other site better illustrates the city's former importance than the vast Antonine Baths (right), built in around 160CE. These were the third largest in the Roman world at nearly 400,000 square feet, with a main Olympic-sized pool and latrines so large they were once thought to be a theater.

Almost certainly the most haunting site at Carthage is that known as the Sanctuary of Tophet where hundreds of stones mark children's graves. Roman-inspired black legends suggest these were babies killed to please the chief deity Ba'al Hammon and the fertility goddess Tanit, but they are more likely to be the result of stillbirths and high infant mortality.

PURA ULUN DANU BATUR
BALI, INDONESIA

Picturesquely located on Batur Lake, this Hindu temple complex is dedicated to a variety of deities but principally to the goddess of lakes and rivers.

Mount Batur is an active volcano and the temple was relocated here, to the crater lake at the highest point, in 1926 after an eruption had destroyed both the village and the older temple at the base. There are nine temples and 285 shrines and pavilions. There is a similar complex called Puru Ulun Danu Bratan (following pages) at Lake Bratan near Badugal: the 11-tiered *meru*, or pagoda-like roof, honors the lake goddess Batari Dewi Ulun Danu, and the three-tiered *meru* honors Ratu Ayu Kentel Gumi, who protects the crops from disease.

The ancient system of water management of the Hindu Balinese involves synchronized irrigation, and the practice is deeply ingrained in the culture. Wherever water is diverted to an agricultural community there is a temple devoted to Dewi Danu, the water goddess, providing a focal point in each village. The basis of a Balinese year is actually the 210-day growing cycle of rice. The success of that depends on flooded terraces to deter pests. The irrigation system distributes the nutrient-rich run-off from Mount Batur—the key to Bali's fertile ecology.

ACROPOLIS OF ATHENS
ATHENS, GREECE

This citadel represents ideals—quests for perfection that have shaped Western civilization.

After the Persians had sacked Athens in 480BCE the Acropolis was a ruin. Rebuilding began in the 440s under Pericles, who declared: "The admiration of the present and succeeding ages will be ours." Within decades great structures once again dominated the outcrop of rock. The Parthenon, Propylaia, and Erechtheion were joined by smaller temples, including one dedicated to Athena Nike, bringer of victory.

However, it was the marble grandeur of the Parthenon, the biggest temple on the mainland, that became legendary—acclaimed as the finest ever Doric temple (although it also served as the treasury of the Delian League). Created in 447–438 by Iktinos and Kallikrates, it was a suitable home for Pheidias's huge new gold and ivory statue of Athene Parthenos, celebrating her virgin (*parthenos*) status. The exterior's sculpted pediments, friezes, and metopes included a Gigantomachy theme that demonstrated the goddess's civilizing influence.

Both impressive and beautiful, the architecture symbolized the core values of Periclean Greece. When viewed from the *agora* in the center of ancient Athens below, the buildings were a reminder that the city was dedicated to higher purposes.

CHÂTEAU DE CHENONCEAU
CHENONCEAUX, FRANCE

In 1512 Thomas Bohier acquired a manor on the north bank of the Cher River. He initiated a rebuild, but it is women who have shaped this building, nicknamed "Château des Dames."

In 1515–1521 Bohier's wife Katherine Briconnet created a Renaissance château, with a retained medieval keep. Acquired by the Valois monarchy as a bad debt, Henri II's mistress, Diane de Poitiers, enhanced its gardens and commissioned Philibert de l'Orme (of Fontainebleau fame) to add a bridge. After Henri's death, his widow Catherine de Medici forced Diane out and then commissioned a two-story grand gallery and ballroom for the bridge. When her son, Francois II, became king the first fireworks display in France was held here.

After Catherine's death in 1589 the castle was neglected. The widow of the assassinated Henry III wandered aimlessly through its corridors for the rest of her days. In the 1700s Louise Dupin saved it from revolutionaries, thanks to the bridge across the river—and during the Second World War the river divided Occupied France and Vichy France, which made the galleried bridge a corridor between the two. Owned by the Menier chocolatier family since 1913, Chenonceau receives about a million visitors each year.

LESHAN GIANT BUDDHA
SICHUAN, CHINA

With a height of 233 feet and a width at the shoulders of about 92 feet, the extraordinary three-dimensional masterpiece at Leshan is the world's largest seated stone *buddha*.

At the insistence of a well-known local monk, work began on this sculpture in 713CE and was completed 90 years later, and subsequently painted. Most Tang-era sculpture is actually to be found in Buddhist grottoes, but the figure at Leshan is carved into the cliffside of Lingyun Shan on the bank of the Min River.

The explanation lies in the treacherous currents to be found here, near the confluence of three rivers, which had drowned many local boatmen. It was believed that the presence of a Maitreya, a unique figure who is both a *bodhisattva* and a *buddha*—the prophesied messiah-like *buddha* of the future age, would save lives (and, of course, bring merit to the donors). Known in Chinese as Mile Fo ("Loving One"), he has been the focus of a number of popular, messianic movements in China's history. In this Chinese form, he is often depicted as a round, happy figure, having absorbed elements of the lucky gods of folk religions. At Leshan, the giant future *buddha* gazes across the river to Mount Emei, which is one of four sacred mountains in Chinese Buddhism. There is a local saying: "The mountain is a *buddha*, and the *buddha* is a mountain."

NEW YORK CITYSCAPE
NEW YORK CITY, USA

Emerging simultaneously in late nineteenth-century Chicago and New York City, "skyscraper" buildings have since transformed our urban space utterly.

New York—and compact Manhattan especially—has been an epicenter of high-rise construction for more than a century, after a combination of safe elevators with iron, steel, or reinforced concrete framing (instead of load-bearing walls) meant that architects and engineers could build ever higher.

Today, the city has more than 200 buildings in excess of 500 feet high. There are classics that immortalize individuals (Woolworth, 1913) and corporations (Chrysler, 1930). The gigantic, 22-acre, art deco development around Rockefeller Plaza (1931–1940), with 19 related buildings, was a visionary attempt to create a community of such structures—and to this day the central "skyscraper alley" area around Fifth and Sixth Avenues is seen by many as Manhattan's architectural heart and soul. More recently, when it is completed One World Trade Center (replacing the "Twin Towers" destroyed in 2001) will be the tallest in the USA, its antenna reaching a symbolic 1,776 feet (the US declared its independence in 1776). Probably the most popular addition to the city's skyline in recent years is the High Line—a park created along the tracks of the disused overhead railroad.

CHRIST THE REDEEMER
RIO DE JANEIRO, BRAZIL

A global icon of the city half a mile below, and visible 20 miles away, this immense art deco statue of Jesus gazes serenely, welcoming visitors with open arms.

Standing atop Corcovado Mountain, this colossus—92 feet fingertip to fingertip—of "Christo Redentor" in soapstone and reinforced concrete was inaugurated in 1931. More than a quarter of a million pilgrims made the journey in the rain to see the unveiling of what was the world's largest statue of Jesus Christ.

The genesis for it dates to the 1850s, when a local priest, Pedro Maria Boss, first sought support for a monument to demonstrate the devotion of Rio's faithful. When public support later grew for a statue, the peace-gesture design of Brazilian Heitor da Silva Costa was selected, to be created by French sculptor Paul-Maximilien Landowski. From 1922 onward, the 700 tons of pieces were moved up the mountain and assembled into the figure standing 98 feet high on top of a 26-feet pedestal.

In 2000 Christ the Redeemer had new lighting, elevators, and escalators installed for the hundreds of thousands of tourists who visit each year. In 2006, to reclaim the sacred sense of the site, the Roman Catholic Church consecrated it as a sanctuary, which means that weddings and baptisms can be conducted in the chapel built in the base.

THE FORBIDDEN CITY
BEIJING, CHINA

The emperor of China lived in a complex of buildings that reflected his supreme status and relationship to cosmic forces. Its high walls kept it off-limits to common people.

Built by the Ming dynasty (1368–1644), the Forbidden City (in Chinese "the Great Within"), now known as the Palace Museum, has about 980 buildings in less than one-third of a square mile, with gates at each cardinal point. Separated by courtyards, the red ocher walls of pavilions and throne rooms have ornate roof beams and rafters beneath glazed tiles of imperial yellow, the ridges and eaves adorned with auspicious creatures, dominated by the dragon. Red was the color thought to bring good fortune, while yellow symbolized earth, represented the Middle Kingdom, and was therefore the imperial color.

Viewed from the Shenwu men (Gate of Divine Prowess) at the northern exit (right), the complex's central north–south axis is apparent. Along it stand the paramount buildings, following the principles of Chinese geomancy. The entire layout reflected the idea that the world was square, with China at its sacred center.

The Forbidden City gets about eight million visitors a year. During the October 2012 national holiday the site drew a record 180,000 people in a day, which meant that more than 350 people were entering every minute.

TAJ MAHAL
AGRA, INDIA

This monument to love was built by the Mughal emperor Shah Jahan (reigned 1627–1658) in memory of his wife, Mumtaz Mahal, who bore him 14 children and died in childbirth.

Erected on the southern bank of the sacred Yamuna River, the mausoleum was begun in 1631 and took 20,000 laborers and craftsmen from India, Persia, and Central Asia nearly two decades to complete. The result is the high point of Indo-Persian tomb building, combining *chatri* pavilions with *iwan* halls and bulbous domes. Dressed in pure, shiny white marble, the building's color varies according to the light, and its perfect proportions embody majesty and serenity in equal measure. The marble represents eternity and the interior decoration— floral themes in relief and semiprecious-stone inlay— symbolizes the beauty and transience of earthly life.

The tomb is reached through the *charbagh*, a four-part garden that represents an earthly vision of Mumtaz's abode in paradise. On the opposite riverbank is the Mahtab Bagh ("Moonlit Garden"). Legend has it that the emperor planned to build a black marble replica tomb for himself. In fact, he is buried alongside his beloved and that garden was probably the perfect viewing spot. Since 2004 limited numbers have been able to enjoy night visits to the Taj Mahal around the time of the full moon.

On a plateau on the coast of Peru are hundreds of earthworked geometrical lines and about 70 figural renderings scraped into the desert. Who made these striking pieces of landscape architecture and why?

The creators were the Nasca, a civilization that lasted until about 700CE and whose heartland was the Nazca River valley. Although the images can be seen from surrounding hillsides, were they made solely for divine eyes or are there other explanations? Their variety, and the lengthy timespan during which the lines (many are pre-Nasca) were made, mean that it is likely there were many reasons.

Some may be culturally significant symbols—such as the hummingbird (right), which Nasca warriors revered for its swiftness. Few match astronomical alignments, but some argue that the lines were ritually swept and that perhaps the intention was to create sacred pathways, which conforms with Andean culture more generally. But perhaps water provided the most powerful motive. The coastal region is arid and the Nasca in particular were skilled at building cisterns and using underground channels, dug into aquifers, to move water to drier areas to support farming. The lines may well be the work of a cult devoted in some ritualistic way to summoning water from the mountains to the valley.

VENETIAN LAGOON
VENICE, ITALY

Although its grandeur is undeniably faded, "La Serenissima" still casts an alluring spell over any visitor—a city that shimmers in a splendid existence between land and sea.

Spread over 118 islands in a 210-square-mile lagoon, Venice has been a maritime power since the tenth century and under the doges (*c.*697–1797) it controlled commerce in the eastern Mediterranean. The wealth from that enabled Venice to become—thanks to its unique setting and the artistic masters who worked there—a peerless architectural gem.

Today, although the more than 20 million tourists who outnumber the 60,000 residents can make it seem a "less-than-serene-one," its sights can still soothe any stresses. Echoing Claude Monet's painting, this silhouette (right) viewed from San Marco Basin is Palladio's basilica of San Giorgio Maggiore (1566–1610).

The city, with its 150 canals (following pages), still wages an endless fight for survival against a merciless sea. To alleviate the increased incidence of flooding the MOSE project was begun in 2003 and is due to complete in 2014: 78 floodgates will be able to stop seawater from pouring in across the three inlets to the lagoon. Hopefully it will preserve this most precious of places—a city whose soundtrack is not the hum of car engines but the gentle lapping of waters.

his defining element
f Toronto's cityscape
also Canada's most
elebrated structure.

pon completion in April
975, Canada's National
CN) Tower became
e world's tallest free-
anding structure (1,815
et), which it remained
ntil it was overtaken by
urj Khalifa in 2007.
In 1994–1995, the
merican Society of Civil
ngineers, searching for
arvellous engineering
chievements that scorned
e notion of "it can't be
one", classified the CN
ower as one of the Seven
Vonders of the Modern
Vorld. Some 1,537
orkers toiled for 24 hours
day, five days a week,
raise the concrete and
eel tower by 18 feet a
ay. The final result was a
ere 1.1 inches off plumb.
The tower was always
esigned as a public
traction as well as a
lecommunications hub.
he SkyPod is a seven-
ory observation structure
at gets about 1.5 million
ternational visitors each
ear. Built around the base,
revolving restaurant
fers views more than
150 feet above the
ty. Six glass-fronted
evators take visitors to
e top. Since 2007 an
ED system has enabled
e tower to light up the
ronto skyline. In 2011
e EdgeWalk was opened
r tethered thrill-seekers
anting to walk around a
feet wide ledge on the
of of the restaurant at
168 feet up—the world's
ghest, full-circle, hands-
ee walk.

STANDING STONES
CARNAC, FRANCE

Quarried thousands of years ago from local granite, the stones at Carnac in Brittany are one of the most impressive of all northwest Europe's megalithic monuments.

Carnac has more than 3,000 *menhir*s (from the Breton *men* or "stone" and *hir* or "long"), which are simple, upright stones of the kind erected mainly during the 3200–1500BCE period, though some date to a millennium earlier than that. The stones are often part of local folklore: for example, a Christian tale that they were pagan soldiers petrified by St. Cornelius; or Romans turned to stone by Merlin.

Although many standing stones can be found in western Europe, in places they command the landscape and appear to be arranged into a form of complex. The Romans seem to have recognized this about Carnac and used its stones for ritual purposes, incising some with images of their own deities. However, the purpose of the originals is unknown—perhaps they were erected in honor of ancestors.

The Carnac stones are nearly all arranged into parallel rows and several main formations or alignments have been identified. The Ménec has 11 rows stretched out for about 3,800 feet. The Kermario has 10 rows that stretch for 4,300 feet. The Kerlescan has 13 but they stretch for only 2,600 feet. The mystery persists.

Producing the shock of the new when it was unveiled, this wrought iron tower now embodies the panache of France's capital city.

In 1889 France commemorated the centenary of its revolution, and the age of science and industry it was felt to have inaugurated, by holding the Paris Exposition. Begun in 1887, the entrance arch to the exposition was a four-pylon tower of malleable metal 985 feet high (it can vary slightly depending on the temperature), which made it the world's tallest structure. It was designed by engineers Maurice Koechlin and Émile Nouguier and embellished by architect Stephen Sauvestre, all working for Gustave Eiffel's company, which was experienced in bridge construction. Eiffel bought the rights.

The network of thousands of beams (following pages) of wrought iron fastened by 2.5 million rivets offered the best strength, flexibility, and wind resistance for least weight—its elasticity enables the top to move back and forth by several inches on a windy day. However, the metal must be repainted every seven years to avoid corrosion.

The tower was only licensed for 20 years, but having proved useful as a telecommunications mast it is now more than 120 years old. About a quarter of a billion people have been up the tower and today seven million more ascend it each year. At night there is a spectacular hourly light show.

DOME OF THE ROCK
JERUSALEM, ISRAEL

Built in 684–691CE for the Umayyad caliph Abd al-Malik (reigned 685–705), the Dome of the Rock is Islam's earliest surviving monument (with the oldest *mihrab*), although its original purpose is unknown.

The dazzling Dome of the Rock is the crowning glory of the al-Haram al-Sharif ("Noble Sanctuary"), or Temple Mount—the former location of the Jewish Temple. The rock itself is the summit where Abraham nearly sacrificed his son, and where the Prophet Muhammad ascended into heaven on his night journey with the angel Gabriel. Jesus preached nearby on the eve of his arrest.

Al-Malik was probably showing that Islam could match the other faiths. The shrine's circular interior is like a Greco-Roman-Byzantine rotunda, with its ornate mosaics and the pillars and arches supporting the dome. Surrounding it are two octagonal ambulatories. The exterior was once sheathed with marble and glass mosaics, like those inside, but in the 1540s Suleiman the Magnificent replaced them with tiles. In 1956–1962 these were replaced by facsimile copies made in Italy.

Beneath the rock is the "Well of Souls," where it is believed the dead meet twice a month to pray. Centuries ago, Muslims who prayed here after circuiting the rock were issued with a certificate that admitted them to paradise, which was to be buried with them.

DELPHI
MOUNT PARNASSOS, GREECE

People from all over the Greek world, including political decision-makers, came to consult the oracle at Panhellenic sanctuaries such as Delphi, which Zeus had established was the navel of the Earth.

The magnificent natural setting at Delphi was where this sacred spot was marked by a carved stone, the *omphalos*. It was kept in the inner sanctum of a temple dedicated to Apollo, who it was believed spoke through the mouth of the priestess known as the Pythia.

A sanctuary was here in the tenth century CE, to which were later added terraces, temples, treasuries, and even a theater and stadium for the Pythian Games. By the eighth century BCE the Pythia was the most authoritative of all Greece's oracles. After a purification ritual, she fell into a trance, before uttering a prophecy.

The best-preserved remains at Delphi stand on the lower part (right). This is the Marmaria sanctuary sacred to Athene Pronaia ("Guardian of the Temple"), where a visitor heading for the temple of Apollo was first expected to offer a sacrifice. The Tholos part dates from slightly later and has had three of its 20 Doric columns restored; its rotunda may evoke the navel of the Earth, but its purpose is unknown. The Romans plundered the site and later closed it because it had lost its meaning with the spread of Christianity.

BONIFACIO
CORSICA, FRANCE

The citadel of Bonifacio roosts on a clifftop, like a watchtower on the lookout for a fresh wave of invaders to follow the Greeks, Romans, Pisans, Genoese, and French.

Located on the island's southern tip, opposite Sardinia, Bonifacio was founded by a Tuscan noble of that name in 828, but people have been living here for much longer. The skeleton of the "dame de Bonifacio" dates to 6570BCE and in the *Odyssey* Homer's description of the Laestrygonian harbor fits the Bonifacio Narrows.

The republic of Genoa left the greatest imprint on Bonifacio after it had conquered Corsica and made the town into a fortress. The resulting labyrinth of narrow streets is entered on foot through the Porte de Genes (Genoa Gate), with its sixteenth-century drawbridge. Some of the characterful medieval buildings are six stories high; others were originally without front doors and entered instead by ladder through the upper floor. The Porte de France (French Gate) was added in 1854, after France had assumed control of the island, and is intended for vehicles. When the French ended the local merchants' privileges, decline set in.

In recent decades the careful restoration of the walled citadel and its rich, culturally diverse mix of atmospheric historical architecture has helped tourism to revive this interesting coastal town.

The capital of Tuscany rose to prominence in the fifteenth century under the Medici banking dynasty. The Renaissance began here and the city is widely acclaimed as one of the world's most beautiful.

The three-arched Ponte Vecchio (right) is a fine medieval (1345) example of a structure that was once common: a bridge with shops. In August 1944 this was the city's only crossing of the River Arno not blown up by retreating German forces, perhaps because they thought it too fragile to bear the weight of Allied armored vehicles.

In a city of exceptional palazzos and piazzas, one of the finest spaces is the spiritual center: the Piazza del Duomo (following pages). The cathedral of Santa Maria del Fiore (1296–1492) there is of huge architectural significance thanks to its dome, a technical *tour de force* engineered by Filippo Brunelleschi in 1420. Also part of the cathedral complex is the bell tower or campanile (1334–1359), partly by Giotto. Located in front of the cathedral is a Romanesque basilica (1059–1128), the octagonal San Giovanni Baptistery, built on top of a Roman temple to Mars. The exterior is finished with geometrically patterned white and green marble, and set in its north and south sides are extraordinary gilded bronze doors by Lorenzo Ghiberti and Andrea Pisano respectively.

HASSAN II MOSQUE
CASABLANCA, MOROCCO

Completed in 1993, the Hassan II Mosque was commissioned by the King of Morocco in 1980 on his sixtieth birthday to provide the city with a landmark monument.

Inspired by a Quranic verse that states "the throne of Allah was built on water," the mosque is on a platform above the sea, where it has a part-glass floor that reveals what lies below. The roof also opens to reveal God's heavenly creation above. As the King had declared: "I want to build this mosque on the water, because God's throne is on the water. Therefore, the faithful who go there to pray, to praise the creator on firm soil, can contemplate God's sky and ocean." The 689-feet-tall minaret is the highest in the world and has lasers installed that can probe the night sky in the direction of Mecca. No expense has been spared and the cost—an estimated 800 million US dollars—was met by public donations.

Although the 50 glass chandeliers came from Murano, Venice, the remainder of the materials were sourced in Morocco: cedar from the Middle Atlas mountains, granite from Tafraoute, and marble from Agadir. Thousands of local craftsmen provided the entire structure with its luxurious decorative embellishment of intricate mosaics, sculpted plasterwork, and carved and painted wood, which is reminiscent of the Moorish architectural treasures of southern Spain.

THE GRAND MOSQUE
MECCA, SAUDI ARABIA

Also known as the Masjid al-Haram, the great mosque in Mecca is the focal point of the *Hajj* each year when millions of the world's Muslims gather there.

There has been a mosque on this site since the seventh century. Until 630 Mecca (Makkah) was important as the site of the Haram, at the heart of which was the Ka'ba, the object of pagan worship among the local Arab tribes. After the triumph of Muhammad's message of Islam, the Ka'ba became a shrine dedicated to Allah (God). The cube-shaped building—the "house"—is believed to have been built by Adam, then rebuilt and purified by Abraham, and purged again (of its pagan idols) by Muhammad.

Every day, Muslims pray in its direction (*qibla*). These prayers are one of the five duties or "pillars" of Islam, as is the making of at least one pilgrimage to Mecca itself, at the climax of which the pilgrim circles the Ka'ba and attempts to kiss the sacred black stone (a remnant of the original) embedded in one corner.

Having been rebuilt many times over the centuries, with minarets added, the historic parts of the current mosque date to the 1570s. It was greatly expanded in the last century by the Saudi kings and the courtyard areas accommodate approximately 800,000 worshippers. A massive expansion project currently underway will increase the holy site's capacity to more than two million people.

HIMEJI CASTLE
HIMEJI, HYOGO, JAPAN

Himeji is the finest surviving example of a vast fortress dating from Japan's tumultuous era of warring feudal lords.

Between 1601 and 1609 Ikeda Terumasa, a vassal of the new *shogun* Tokugawa Ieyasu, built this castle, which dominated the area until the Meiji era in 1868.

The well-preserved main keep, with its undulating gables and dormers, is made of wood, finished with earthen plaster and painted white. Symbolic fire-prevention was provided by ridge-tiles in the form of abstract fish.

This shapely form has led to the nickname "White Heron" because it appears ready for flight. However, it is a mistake to equate elegance with fragility: this stronghold has deterred attackers and withstood major earthquakes. Three water-filled moats prevented a rapid attack or siege. The six-story keep and smaller towers lie at the heart of a spiral of enclosing walls, with many slits from which to fire. The outermost stone walls are 50 feet high and sloping.

As well prepared as it was, Himeji was never actually in a battle. In 1871 a local man bought it for 23 yen (then at parity with the US dollar) in order to develop the land, but he found the demolition costs prohibitive—and so the castle survived unscathed. Finally, in 1931 it was designated a national treasure, and in the 1950s and 1960s it was restored. Today, it is a popular attraction, hosting a cherry blossom festival each year.

MASADA
DEAD SEA, ISRAEL

This mountain plateau redoubt, high above the Judean Desert, was once a palace complex built for King Herod. It has become famous as the site of a last stand by the Zealots—Jewish resisters to Rome during the revolt of 66–73CE.

By 70 the Zealots at Masada were the final Jewish resisters. Jerusalem had been sacked and the Temple destroyed. In 72 the Tenth Legion set up eight camps below, connected by a seven-mile-long siege wall, and began to construct a huge camp (still visible to the far right, opposite) for the final assault. With defeat appearing inevitable, leader Eleazar Ben Yair supposedly told the 960 occupants: "… a glorious death is preferable to a life of infamy." All but two took their own lives. After a fifth-century Christian monastic community had departed the by then earthquake-damaged hilltop, Masada lay deserted for 1,300 years, until rediscovered in the 1820s. Excavations finally began in the 1960s. The entire site now lies in a National Park within the Judean Desert Nature Reserve. As a symbol of Jewish national identity, Masada is a popular attraction and a new visitor center opened in 2000, which can handle a million visitors annually. A 1970s' cable car has been replaced by a less intrusive system linking the center to the summit, although arduous historic routes remain in use for walkers.

VOLUBILIS
MOROCCO

This North African city was once the capital of the independent kingdom of Mauretania, which became a client of Rome after the destruction of Carthage in 149–146BCE. Today, it is the most impressive Roman site in Morocco.

Volubilis became the administrative center for the Roman province of Mauretania Tingitana. It lay in an agriculturally rich area, which explains the remains of about a hundred premises used for olive oil production in the town, and has all the hallmarks of Roman development: roads, baths, temples, an aqueduct, a Forum, Basilica (right), and a Capitol (following pages). The structures date from the early centuries CE. The main road, the *decumanus maximus*, leads to a triumphal arch built in 217 for Emperor Caracalla, the same year he was assassinated.

The city is one of the few places where Roman mosaics can be viewed in situ and there are about 30 fine examples in more than a dozen mansions, including the House of Orpheus, House of the Ephèbe, House of Venus, and House of Dionysus.

A new visitor center is under construction, which is being embedded discretely into the overlooking hillside. The historic atmosphere here is palpable and it provided Martin Scorsese with a fine location for scenes in his 1988 film *The Last Temptation of Christ*.

NOTRE-DAME BASILICA
MONTRÉAL, CANADA

This ornate church was built between 1824 and 1829 in Gothic Revival style—the first such example in Canada. For about half a century, Notre-Dame was the largest house of worship in North America.

From the early 1870s, Victor Bourgeau, one of Quebec's leading architects, oversaw a decade-long romantic phase of decoration at Notre-Dame. This was inspired by the Gothic masterpiece of Sainte-Chapelle in Paris, built in the thirteenth century to house the relics of King Louis IX of France. During a trip to Europe, Curé Victor Rousselot had been awed by its use of light, stained glass and the sensory effect created by combinations of color, including gold and azure. Notre-Dame's gold stars on a blue background derive directly from that Parisian example.

Equally sumptuous is the sanctuary altarpiece (right), the theme of which is sacrifice. Four Old Testament scenes of ritual offerings complement the centerpiece of Jesus' crucifixion. In the upper section, Christ, conqueror of death through his resurrection, crowns his mother, the Blessed Virgin (Our Lady), in heaven. Raised to the status of minor basilica in 1982, Notre-Dame also stages a popular multimedia sound and light show on many evenings throughout the year and hosts classical music concerts during the summer.

STATUE OF LIBERTY
NEW YORK CITY, USA

A century ago, New York harbor was the gateway to the New World. Millions of Europeans were welcomed by this female colossus, which is inscribed beneath with the lines: "Give me your tired, your poor, your huddled masses yearning to breathe free..."

At 305 feet high from the ground to the tip of the torch, "Liberty Enlightening the World" was the city's tallest structure when it was unveiled in 1886. She stands amid broken shackles and her crown's rays represent the seven seas and continents.

Popularly known as the Statue of Liberty, she was a belated gift from France for the centennial of the American Revolution: the tablet she holds reads "JULY IV MDCCLXXVI" (July 4, 1776). The pedestal was by American Richard Morris Hunt and the figure was by French sculptor Frédéric-Auguste Bartholdi. A 350-piece iron skeleton made in Paris by Gustave Eiffel enables the structure to sway in a gust. The figure is dressed in thin copper sheeting, which has weathered to its distinctive patina.

In 1986 the statue was restored and the torch now has a modified flame design covered with sheets of pure gold.

Given originally to mark an international friendship forged through revolution, the statue has become a symbol of the human desire for democracy, freedom from oppression, and opportunity for all.

CITADEL OF BUKHARA
BUKHARA, UZBEKISTAN

These bulging walls belong to the ark—a clay-built fortress that dates back to the early centuries CE in Bukhara, a center for East-West commerce along the Silk Road in Central Asia.

The ark is the city's oldest monument and it has been destroyed—by the Mongols, among others—and rebuilt many times. By the twentieth century, before their overthrow by revolutionaries in 1920, the emir of Bukhara had turned the ark into a city within the city, with a treasury, mosques, and palace.

Much of the compound's interior has disappeared, and, despite restorations, part of the ark's walls collapsed in both 2011 and 2012. The walls need wooden beams to hold the packed clay and infill materials together, and it is thought that corruption may have led to insufficient timber being used.

The ark had a jail, but it was the *zindan*, just outside the ark, that was notorious. Its "bug pit" dungeon was infested with deadly insects and prisoners did not usually last long. In 1842, the era of the Great Game, two British officers, Colonel Stoddart and Captain Conolly, were thrown into the "bug pit," which they survived—albeit only to be forced to dig their own graves in front of the ark, before being beheaded as spies. Missionary Joseph Wolff made their story public after going to the city to discover their fate. The *zindan* can still be visited, together with the torture chamber.

CHURCH OF ST. GEORGE
LALIBELA, ETHIOPIA

Built in about 1220, this remarkable cruciform church is a memorial to a devout monarch who is recognized as a saint in the Ethiopian Orthodox Tewahedo Church.

The Church of St. George (Bete Giyorgis in Amharic) is the last of a group of monolithic churches that were created in the highlands of Ethiopia. King Lalibela believed that God had asked him to make a holy place of pilgrimage and devotion—a "New Jerusalem" to rival sacred Axum (Aksum). After ten churches, he abdicated and became a hermit; his widow commissioned St. George's).

Excavating up to 40 feet down into the volcanic bedrock was a time-consuming and labor-intensive process—thus tradition has it that angels worked the night shift, carving twice as fast as humans could. Evidence suggests that only the finest churches were built in the 1200s; the others already existed in some form and were converted for ecclesiastic use.

There are two groups of churches, either side of a seasonal river, known as the Jordan. Lalibela may have created an alternative form of pilgrimage to Jerusalem because of Saladin's control of the holy city after 1187—we will never know. Lalibela remains a popular place of pilgrimage, with many Ethiopians drawn to the king's tomb in Bete Golgotha, and visitors from around the world attracted by the rock-cut churches.

he ruined city-state f Palenque, which njoyed a golden age nder Pacal ("Shield," eigned 615–683CE), testament to the reative genius that nce held sway here.

he buildings are more legant than elsewhere in he Maya lowlands, and vere once adorned with lue- and red-painted tucco reliefs depicting oyal genealogies—most aving been built for Pacal r his son Chan-Bahlum "Snake-Jaguar").

The palace (right, center) hat dominates the city lates from the seventh nd eighth centuries. It consists of long, single-tory rooms around patios, nd a perimeter with galleries. The purpose of he three-story tower—the only square tower in the egion—is unknown, though ome scholars speculate hat it may have been an stronomical observatory.

As he neared the end of his life, Pacal ordered his own funerary monument o be built: the Temple of he Inscriptions (far right), where he was buried in a magnificent sarcophagus.

Pacal's son built three pyramid temples (top eft) that echo the distant mountains: the Temple of he Cross, the Temple of he Foliated Cross, and the Temple of the Sun. Each contains many carvings and texts telling the Maya story of creation.

Much of this "forest of kings" is unexcavated. Haunting and mysterious, many visitors must wonder what more remains to be discovered.

This city was once known as Mogador and for centuries it has been a thriving port and a center of trade.

In ancient times the city made its living from fishing, especially the production of *garum* paste, and the industry that produced the purple dye so highly valued in Rome. This dye was made using the murex mollusc found among the offshore Purpuraire islands.

In 1765 Sultan Sidi Muhammad ibn Abdallah commissioned Nicholas Théodore Cornut, from Avignon in France, to rebuild the city's fifteenth-century fortifications, which dated from when the Portuguese had occupied Essaouira, before they abandoned it in 1541. Cornut's defensive ramparts and his esplanade (the Skala) are in Vauban's style, but they blend harmoniously and atmospherically with the North African architecture.

The attractive *medina* of Essaouira includes several old town gates, an integrated *kasbah*, the bastions of Bab Doukkala and Bab Marrakech, and the characterful former Jewish quarter called the *mellah*. The sultan made Essaouira an open city, attracting an ethnically diverse population who made it into a thriving commercial hub, with Jews in particular given favorable royal merchant status.

Only after independence in the twentieth century was the city's name changed to Essaouira, which means "well walled" in Arabic.

SHATRUNJAYA HILLS
GUJARAT, INDIA

This temple-city near Palitana in western India is a pilgrimage site for the largest sect in Jainism, the Shvetambara ("white-clad"), and one of the few areas in India where Jainism remains a vibrant faith.

Jains believe that every living creature houses an immortal soul and take great care to avoid injury to anything. Through ascetic practices, Jains hope to purify the soul, a goal considered to be the ultimate purpose of life on Earth. Jainism has 24 teachers, from Adinath ("First Lord"), to Mahavira ("Great Hero"). Called *tirthankara*s ("ford-builders"), they laid Jainism's spiritual path.

Each year about 400,000 Jains visit Shatrunjaya Hills (right), one of five key Jain holy places. Shatrunjaya means "conquering the enemies"—a reference to undesirable passion, sin, and suchlike. The site dates back a thousand years, but most of the buildings are from recent centuries. There are more than 800 glistening marble temples, dedicated to each of the *tirthankara*s, built on its two summits, which is probably the world's largest temple complex.

Jains believe the hills were sanctified by Adinath, who delivered his first sermon here. He is celebrated in the most conspicuous temple on the site, which is the most auspicious place to end the *varsitap* ("year-long fast") marked by the Akshay Tritiiya festival in spring.

ROYAL MOSQUE
ISFAHAN, IRAN

Proclaiming the emergence of Isfahan as a splendid new capital city filled with architectural marvels, this masterpiece of the Safavid dynasty period (1501–1722) is arguably the city's finest building.

The Masjid-i Shah ("Royal Mosque," now Mosque of the Imam, built 1612–1638) anchors the south side of the Maidan-i Naqsh-I Jahan ("World Imitating Square," now Imam Square). This colossal rectangle (1,312 feet by 476 feet), lined all the way round with a double arcade of shops, was the key element in the scheme of urban renewal initiated by Shah Abbas I (reigned 1587–1629) when he moved his capital here from Qazvin in 1590. The square was built to shift the focus away from the old town, with its existing congregational (Friday) mosque, and placed in close proximity to Iran's three sources of power: shah, merchants, and clergy.

The mosque's dominant element is its onion dome, which crowns the prayer hall beneath. The dome was added only after the new building had settled for two years—its vivid blue offering a contrast to the unadorned sand-colored elevations. The tile pattern was made possible by a new enameling technique called "seven colors" (*haft-rangi*) in which the tile was painted a variety of colors, each separated by an oily substance that disappeared during the firing.

8

AMER FORT
AMER, INDIA

The Amer, or Amber, Fort is a citadel near Jaipur, the capital of Rajasthan. Begun in 1592 but not completed until the eighteenth century, the structure was built for Raja Man Singh, a Hindu king of Amer, who ruled from 1590 to 1614.

Situated on a rocky ridge, this fortress served as the seat of the rulers of Rajasthan. Initially, the martial clans of the Rajput Hindu ruling families provided the resistance to the new Mughal empire, but Akbar the Great (reigned 1556–1605) was able to create a ruling class that transcended religious differences. Raja Man Singh actually served as a leading general of the Mughal emperor.

The forbidding fortified exterior (with tall walls and high-up windows) contains a sprawling complex of courtyards, gateways, halls, gardens, palaces, apartments, temples, and pillared pavilions (such as the Diwan-e-Aam public audience hall, the top of which is visible here, right), many of which are lavishly decorated. Many narrow stairways can be defended by small numbers of swordsmen and ridged ramps enable cavalry to move about within.

The fort is a sandstone-and-marble fusion of two architectural styles: the refined inner rooms are characteristically Mughal, but the palace complexes are faithfully Hindu in style.

PERSEPOLIS
FARS, IRAN

Before it was looted and burned by Alexander the Great in 330BCE, this city was the greatest monument of the age, bearing influences from Assyria, Greece, Egypt, and Babylon.

Darius the Great (reigned 522–486BCE) began the building of this new royal city in 518 as an alternative to the capital at Pasargadae, founded by Cyrus the Great. Erected on a series of terraces cut into the base of Mount Rahmat, the well-preserved ruins provide a tantalizing glimpse of the imperial Achaemenid glory that once emanated from here.

Square propylons and tall, multi-columned halls and palaces must have impressed on the visitor that they were in the presence of a mighty ruler to whom they should pay homage. A magnificent terrace stairway, decorated with ornate reliefs and broad enough for royalty and nobles on horseback to ascend side by side, leads to the first palace, where 10,000 people could be accommodated.

Although it is normal for columns to be looted for use elsewhere, it is possible that many here were of cedar or teak rather than stone.

After its destruction the city was lost to time. Known to locals only as "the place of the 40 columns" (for those that remained standing), it was not until the seventeenth century that it was identified as Persepolis. Excavations began less than a century ago.

PIAZZA DEL DUOMO
PISA, ITALY

Their marble whiteness changing in the light and accentuated by the green of the grassy piazza, the medieval buildings in this square constitute one of the world's most famous groups of monuments.

The piazza contains four great structures: the Campo Santo cemetery (background, left), the baptistery (not shown), the cathedral, and the freestanding campanile. Each is quite different, but given a stylistic unity by their open arcades and marble-inlay decoration.

Consecrated in 1118, the cathedral is a triumph of harmonious proportions and delicate ornamentation. The west front (right), with its colored stones, maiolica, and tiered galleries is a façade of real beauty. The elliptical dome over the transept crossing was added in 1380.

By far the most famous edifice is the 200-feet-high "leaning tower" (1173–1370). Closed to the public in 1990, it reopened in 2001 after a decade of engineering work to extract soil from the north side's foundations. This reduced the lean by 20 inches (to 13 feet). Beforehand, computer models had not been able to replicate its 5.5 degrees off perpendicular, collapsing on reaching 5.44 degrees. The explanation lay in the tower's mass of about 16,000 tons. The tilt is now about 4 degrees. It could have been brought back to vertical, but where is the attraction in that?

INLE STUPAS
YWAMA, INLE LAKE, BURMA

This freshwater lake in the Shan region of eastern Burma (Myanmar) is home to the Inth ("people of the lake") and their distinctive ecosystem.

The Inth are devout Buddhists and the lake has many pagodas and a number of monasteries. Nga Hpe Chaung is a wooden monastery out on the open lake, built around more than 600 teak pillars, some gilded within the building's interior. Built in the 1850s, it houses golden statues of the Buddha but is more famous to tourists for its cats trained to jump through hoops for food.

Burmese Buddhist architecture employs brick and stucco painted white to give the impression of stone—such as these (right) distinctive pyramid-bell pagodas at Ywama, many of them crowned by bells that tinkle in the breeze. In the third century CE, King Thiri Dhamma Thawka reputedly built 84,000 pagodas. Hpaung Daw U Pagoda, the main one on the lake, is the focus for a festival held every fall.

The Inth live mainly in villages of houses built on wooden piles driven into the bed of the shallow lake, and they travel about using boats propelled by leg-led rowing (to get a standing view of the lake's entangling weeds). But arguably more interesting is the lake's highly productive floating farmland—dried weed bedding and hyacinth held in place using bamboo sticks.

HE GREAT MOSQUE
ENNÉ, MALI

**built generation after
eneration, this mosque
the largest building
the world to be made
ut of mud—stunning,
cological, sustainable
rchitecture from sub-
aharan Africa.**

am reached the people
sub-Saharan Africa
ong the region's major
ade routes. Djenné is
here savannah meets
esert and there has been
adobe mosque here
nce at least 1330. An
rly nineteenth-century
ccount of the mosque
ggests it was in disrepair
d overrun by thousands
nesting swallows, which
why the then colonial
dministration instigated a
build and a new mosque
thin a year—completed
1907.

Djenné's current Friday
osque, or Great Mosque,
Sahelian vernacular style
a large scale, similar to
cal Dogon buildings. The
nnacles (right) may derive
om a form of ancestral
llar that were symbols of
eation and fertility.

The mosque is effectively
huge hollow termite
ound. Its greatest enemy
the elements, which is
y it stands on a plinth
protect it from floods.
e mud in the walls has
be densely packed to
ve height to the colossal
naret towers. Structural
egrity comes from the
affolding of horizontal
lmwood beams, which
otrude from the façade.
Each year there is a
osque makeover" when
ople come together to
ply new coats of mud
d repair the damage
ne by both rain and sun.

CHÂTEAU DE CHAMBORD
CHAMBORD, FRANCE

A masterpiece of the French Renaissance, the royal château at Chambord in the Loire Valley is an extravagant example of a building with a hybrid character, combining a French feudal-medieval concept with Italian symmetry.

In 1519 work began on a dream castle for King Francois I near the game-rich Sologne forests. The King spent lavish amounts on the property, which was probably designed by Italian Domenico da Cortona. By 1537 the result was an ornate, architecturally flamboyant structure with a 420-feet façade, 440 rooms (many adorned with Francois's salamander motif or his monogram), 365 fireplaces, 800 sculpted capitals, and more than 80 staircases—accompanied by more than 5,400 hectares of woodland. One of the highlights of the château is a double-helix, openwork spiral staircase that allows someone to ascend without being seen by anyone descending—an ingenious design popularly attributed to Leonardo da Vinci, who had been living in France under the king's protection. The stairs end at the roof terrace, which bristles with cupolas, chimneys, pinnacles, and turrets. Despite the effort and expense, the king spent only about two months there during his reign (1515–1547). Curiously, nearly 500 years after it was built, Chambord has only been inhabited for 20 years.

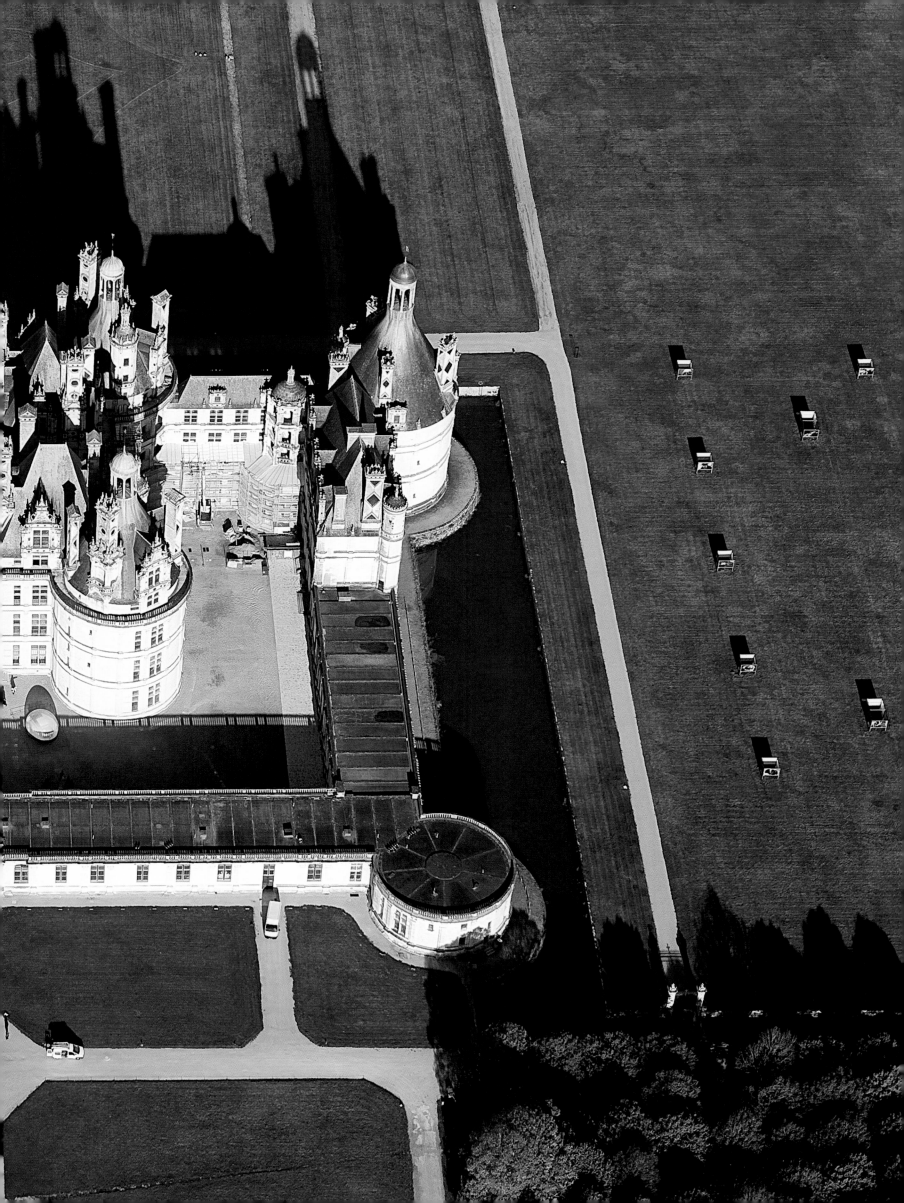

THE GREAT WALL
CHINA

Known as the *wanli changcheng* ("The Wall of Ten Thousand *Li*," which really means 'infinitely long'), this structure is not really one wall but an extensive defensive network dating back to the First Emperor of Qin (reigned 221–210BCE).

Built originally out of stamped earth with watchtowers and barracks at intervals along its length, this chain of fortifications once stretched from the Bay of Bohai in the east to the Jade Gate in the desert of Gansu to the west, some 3,700 miles away. However, because it was discontinuous, it could be—and was—bypassed. A recent (2012) official survey puts the combined length of all the separate parts at an incredible 13,000 miles. Today, the gravest threats are posed not by the horsemen of the steppes but by rain, sandstorms, and relentless mass tourism.

The wall follows the undulating landscape, blending harmoniously and Taoistically with its surroundings. Many dynasties have rebuilt sections, and Mutianyu and the Badaling hills north of Beijing are two of the best-known parts, dating from the Ming period (1368–1644). The battlemented stone sections, using mortar made from rice flour, have paved roads on the upper levels. In June 2012 further sections were opened to avert damage caused by people entering restricted areas.

TEMPLE OF HATSHEPSUT
DEIR EL-BAHRI, EGYPT

This impressive funerary temple, emerging from a bay in the limestone cliffs, was built by a female pharaoh who donned kingly regalia and wielded total power, supported by the priests of Amun at Thebes.

Queen Hatshepsut (reigned c.1479–c.1458BCE) built her temple next to the smaller one (left) that was its inspiration: Nebhepetre Mentuhotep II's mortuary complex, from 500 years earlier. The setting at Deir el-Bahri is dramatic—the Nile floodplain abruptly giving way to the rugged, sacred Theban mountains.

Hatshepsut's graceful monument—called Djeser Djeseru ("Sublime of Sublimes")—is set in a series of colonnaded terraces and access ramps. Fragrant trees, including frankincense, once flanked the central forecourt. It was here, in 1997, that terrorists killed 62 people in a horrific attack. Having recovered its popularity, the site now has a strong security presence. In 2009 a visitor center opened and everything has been atmospherically floodlit.

The Valley of the Kings and Valley of the Queens are on the other side of the cliffs. The queen had two tombs there, but neither had a mummy. Thutmose III may have been responsible—he is known to have erased evidence of a female in the lineage. However, in 2007 remains from a non-royal tomb were confirmed as Egypt's greatest female ruler.

COLOGNE CATHEDRAL
COLOGNE, GERMANY

Although the Kölner Dom's foundation stone was laid in 1248, most of this cathedral was not built until 1840–1880, 632 years later.

A Christian structure had existed on this site since the fourth century, but it was the gift in 1164 of the relics of the three *magi*, or Wise Men, presented to the archbishop by the Holy Roman Emperor Frederick Barbarossa, that meant Cologne became a place of pilgrimage. The archbishop decided to build the greatest cathedral in the Holy Roman Empire. Initially, the work proceeded quickly, but after the Gothic choir had been consecrated in 1322 it slowed and by 1530 lack of both funds and interest meant it had stopped, although a roof was added to weatherproof it.

However, in the nineteenth century a combination of civic support, lottery fund-raising, the Prussian state, and enthusiasm for the Gothic Revival led to a resumption—following the form in the original plans, but using modern methods. For example, the roof truss above the choir is iron rather than wood.

Dedicated to saints Peter and Mary, the twin-tower cathedral is the biggest in Germany, as well as the tallest Gothic church in the world, attracting millions of visitors a year. The golden reliquary remains its greatest treasure, but another significant attraction is the Gero Cross (*c.*976), which is the oldest crucifix in northern Europe.

SHWEDAGON PAGODA
RANGOON, BURMA

Towering 326 feet above a forest of nature spirit shrines, the gleaming Shwedagon in Rangoon (Yangon) elegantly blends Indian and Sri Lankan *stupa* elements into a fluidly tapering Burmese pagoda design.

The majestic Shwedagon ("golden hills") is on top of Singuttara Hill and is the holiest of Burma's Buddhist shrines. It was built to house the relic of hairs donated by the Buddha to two merchants, who were told to enshrine it on a hill where the Buddha said that relics of previous *buddha*s were buried. When they did so, gems are said to have miraculously rained down.

A structure is known to have been on the site in the eleventh century, and the custom of gilding the pagoda began in the late fifteenth century. Over the centuries it has been repeatedly damaged by earthquakes and then renovated, enlarged, and embellished with more and richer decoration by a succession of rulers.

In 1768 the top of the pagoda was brought down and the current structure dates from that rebuild. Thousands of gold bars have been used to provide the genuinely golden glow, and beyond the gaze of the naked eye the upper part is set with precious stones, including 5,448 diamonds, 2,317 rubies and sapphires, 1,065 golden bells, and—at the very top of the seven-tiered decorated spire known as the *hti*—a single 76-carat diamond, added in 1871.

PIŠ CASTLE
PIŠSKÉ PODHRADIE,
LOVAKIA

Wrapped around the
ock at an elevation
f more than 650 feet
bove the surrounding
rea, which lies astride
ncient trading routes,
he castle at Spiš is
ne of Europe's greatest
ortress complexes.

Celtic and then Slavic
ill-forts established this
lace as a focal point in
he region, and although
 has been a ruin for two
enturies this vast site,
ith an area of nearly
alf a million square feet,
till casts a spell over its
urroundings. The castle
was begun in the twelfth
entury and was then
ought over incessantly
y feudal lords. In 1241 it
ithstood a Tartar siege
nd in 1312 the most
owerful noble of the day,
latúš Cák Trenciansky,
ailed to conquer the
astle. Frequent exposure
 battle resulted in many
odifications to the
efenses over the years, as
ell as additions in Gothic
nd Renaissance style.
 Several prominent
amilies owned Spiš,
ncluding the Habsburgs.
lowever, in 1780 a fire
rompted the Csáky family
 abandon the castle
nd build manor houses
 the local villages, often
sing stone salvaged
rom Spiš. Eventually the
astle became a ruin,
vhich was acquired by the
tate in 1945 and became
 national monument
 1961. Today, after
estoration work, there is a
useum and the castle's
ower courtyard, ramparts,
nd barbican are open to
he public.

NEUSCHWANSTEIN CASTLE
BAVARIA, GERMANY

The epitome of a fairytale castle, this nineteenth-century Romantic confection was built so that a king could withdraw from his public. Ironically, today it attracts well over a million visitors a year.

King Ludwig II of Bavaria (reigned 1864–1886) was an eccentric ruler who commissioned some extravagant buildings. Because his real-life political power was limited, the architectural structures Ludwig ordered may have provided him with a "kingdom" where he could act like a real ruler, albeit in a fantasy realm.

Ludwig intended to rebuild Hohenschwangau, his father's castle near the Pöllat Gorge, "in the authentic style of the old German knights' castles." He loved swans as a boy and was later obsessed with the music of Richard Wagner, telling the composer that the castle would remind him of "Tannhäuser" and "Lohengrin," as if it would be an operatic setting. The result, he promised, would be such that the gods will "come to live with us on the lofty heights, breathing the air of heaven."

The castle was begun in 1869 and topped out in 1880, its brick walls clad in limestone. The name Neuschwanstein ("New Swan Rock") was only used after the king's death—for him it was always New Hohenschwangau. The castle was a strong influence on Walt Disney.

THE GREAT MOSQUE
CÓRDOBA, SPAIN

Officially a cathedral today, the congregational mosque popularly known as La Mezquita is the finest surviving artistic achievement of the Spanish Umayyads.

Begun in 786 by the ruler of Córdoba, Abd ar-Rahman, this building survives as an example of Islamic architecture in a city that, under its caliphs, attained a level of sophistication exceeded in Europe and the Islamic world only by Constantinople and Baghdad. Reflecting the dynasty's Syrian roots, the *mihrab* faces Damascus rather than Mecca.

A courtyard of orange trees outside is matched for size inside by a huge prayer hall. Within its 19 lengthwise bays, 850 jasper and granite columns, and 400 horseshoe arches in double-tiered arcades form a spellbinding forest. Magnifying these sensual delights are the stripes of color from wedge-shaped stones (voussoirs) in red brick and pale limestone.

After the recapture of the city in 1236 the mosque was consecrated as a cathedral. It then remained largely untouched for almost three centuries until, against the wishes of the people of Córdoba, the building of a cathedral within was approved. Until recent years this building was a symbol of East–West fusion, but campaigners who want to reopen it to Muslim prayer have provoked a debate about La Mezquita's place in a changing Spain.

POMPEII
POMPEII, ITALY

When Mount Vesuvius erupted in 79ᴄᴇ, most of the town's citizens fled. The 2,000 or so who made the fateful decision to remain now form part of an incredible urban tableau, frozen in time.

Those hoping to sit out the cataclysm were suffocated by ash and poisonous gas, then buried in pumice and tuff for nearly 1,700 years. In 1738 Pompeii was uncovered, much of it intact, from cobblestoned streets (right)—with stepping stones (to avoid the sewage)—to a complex water supply. There are the apartments of poor people and the luxurious mansions of the wealthy, such as the House of the Faun and the House of Menander, with colorful wall paintings. As well as the familiar-seeming temples, baths, and amphitheater (where 60 gladiators died in their barracks on the day), there are also domestic shrines, shops, taverns, snack bars, and a brothel.

Preserved excrement has even revealed what Romans ate and how healthy they were. Thousands of ordinary objects and graffiti, love messages, and political slogans provide fascinating insights into daily life, culture, and customs in a Roman provincial town.

Pompeii's rapid eclipse actually helped to preserve it for posterity—and its power to fascinate us remains undimmed: each year about two million people visit this evocative window into the past.

GOLDEN GATE BRIDGE
SAN FRANCISCO, USA

This steel-cabled bridge, with art deco details and a 4,200-feet-long suspension span, crosses the strait at the entrance to San Francisco Bay from the Pacific Ocean to connect the city with Marin County.

The strait was named "Golden Gate" in 1846 by Captain John C. Frémont, who said that it reminded him of Istanbul's "Golden Horn." There had been proposals for bridges before, but by the 1920s the ferry congestion was intolerable. It took until the 1930s for political obstacles to be overcome, and in 1933, financed by a bond issue, work began under chief engineer Joseph B. Strauss. In November 1936 the two sections of the main span were joined and in April 1937 the last rivet went in. When it opened in May, Wills O'Brien wrote in the *San Francisco Chronicle*: "A necklace of surpassing beauty was placed about the lovely throat of San Francisco yesterday."

The bridge is painted vermilion because the warm color blends well in the setting and improves visibility in a bay prone to advection fog, which forms around the bridge when the humid air from the ocean 220 feet below meets the chilly current flowing parallel to the coast. The structure is crossed each year by about 41 million vehicles and has only been closed three times due to the weather (gusting winds).

MEDINA OF SOUSSE
SOUSSE, TUNISIA

Formerly held by the Phoenicians, Romans, Vandals, and Byzantines, who called it Justinianopolis, the town was renamed Susa by the Arabs when they first arrived in the seventh century.

Rebuilt upon those ancient foundations, this Tunisian town is a fine example of historic Islamic urban development—one dominated by its coastal defenses, because the Arabs of the Aghlabid period (*c.*800–909) feared an assault by Norman Christians from Sicily. The *medina* is encircled by more than a mile of walls, built from the 850s onward on Byzantine fortifications. The blocks of dressed stone were recycled from Roman structures elsewhere. Two of the original six gates survive, as well as the 100-feet-high Khalaf Tower (center), built in 859.

The *kasbah*, or fortress, dates from the eleventh century, and it absorbed the tower, which replaced the *nador*, or watchtower, in the ninth-century *ribat* as the town's main defensive lookout point.

Sousse's *ribat* was both a military and a religious building; the men who lived in it originally would have been *marabout*, which means "holy men." From here, in 827, these warriors—devotees of a conservative brand of Islam—left to conquer Sicily for the Aghlabid emir.

TRAJAN'S ARCH
IMGAD, ALGERIA

Preserved for centuries by sand, the "Pompeii of Africa" was founded by Emperor Trajan in around 100CE as a bulwark against the rebellious Berbers in the Aurès mountains.

A new colony in a key location, Colonia Marciana Ulpia Traiana Thamugadi, named by Trajan in honor of his parents and sister, was built largely for Roman army veterans of the Legion III Augusta, who might be called on should the grain supply to Rome be threatened.

The city's remains provide a fine example of a planned urban grid. The square center, bisected by the north–south and east–west main streets, contains the Forum, a large, open-air theater, a significant number of baths, a large library, a basilica, and the Capitoline Temple, which form the key group of buildings, alongside houses, shops, and taverns.

Designed originally for about 10,000 people, the city soon spread beyond its original footprint. The western gate, along the *decumanus maximus*, was then replaced by the 40-feet-high Trajan's Arch (right), which connects the older and newer parts of the city. The side arches were for pedestrians and the central arch for chariots.

Until recently an international music festival was held each summer in the Roman theater. In 2010 a replica theater was opened at Batna to protect the ancient monument.

LA SAGRADA FAMÍLIA
BARCELONA, SPAIN

The Church of the Holy Family, better known as La Sagrada Família, is famous as the cathedral that was unfinished at the time of Antoni Gaudí's death in 1926.

Gaudí took over the project in 1883, and dedicated his life to realizing a vision that united nature, sacred scripture, and the liturgy. He intended the structure, and not just its detail, to be an allegory of Christianity.

There are three façades, representing Jesus' birth, death, and resurrection (Nativity, Passion, and Glory). The Passion façade (right) was planned in 1911, but only built in 1954–1976. It faces west and sunset, with its symbolic shadows. Its three entrances are dedicated to faith, hope, and charity, and the four bell towers to James the Less, Bartholomew, Thomas, and Philip.

When complete the church will have 18 bell towers to represent the 12 apostles, the four evangelists, the Virgin Mary, and Christ. The soaring spires, achieved without internal or external supports, and the masses of columns within the naves have fluid forms, like a forest (following pages). The organic shapes of the natural world were one of Gaudí's greatest influences—and this expressive, structurally daring, church architecture uses color, texture, geometry, and asymmetry like a giant form of nature.

In November 2010 Pope Benedict XVI consecrated the building as a basilica.

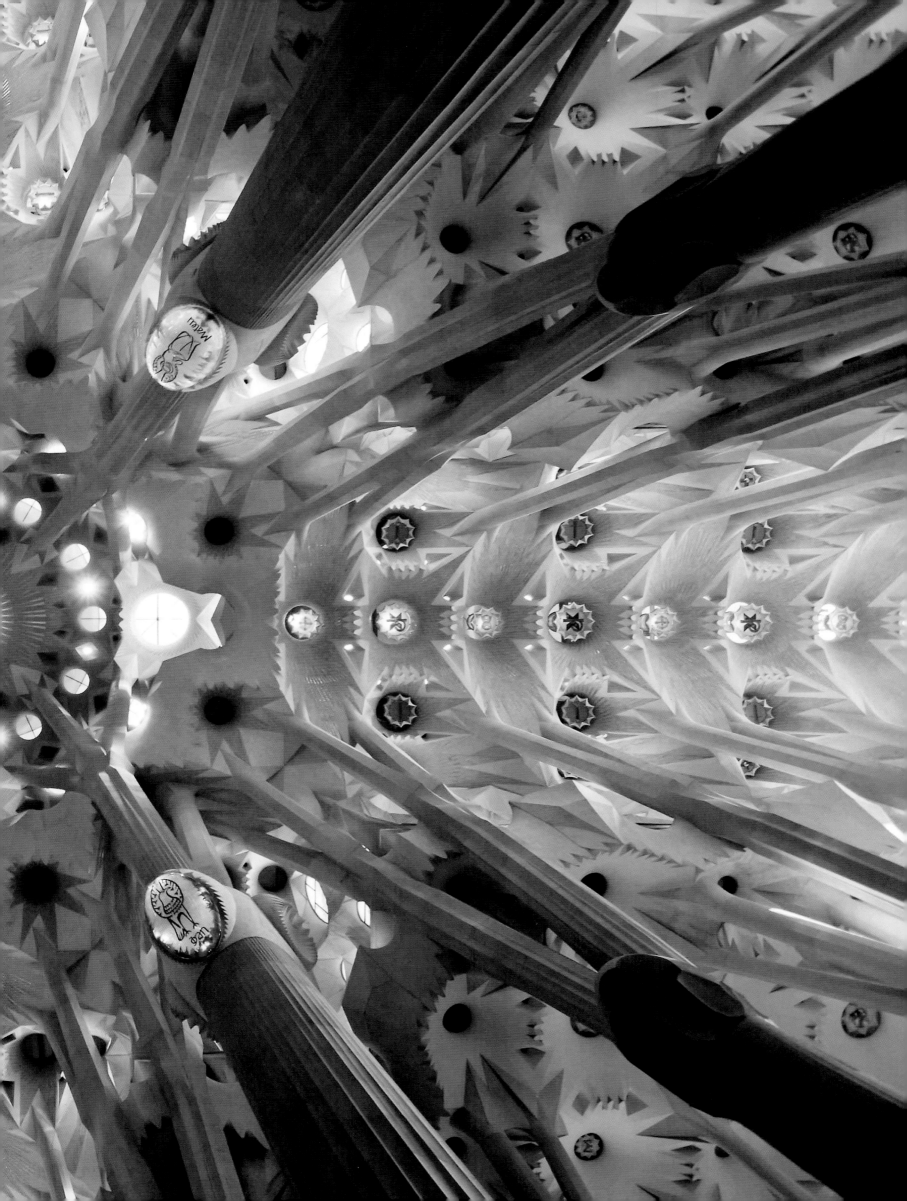

BURJ KHALIFA
DUBAI, UNITED ARAB EMIRATES

Just a generation ago there was only empty desert sand. Today, Burj Khalifa dominates the "Downtown Dubai" development, which includes a vast mall and fountain. For the first time since 1311, when Lincoln's cathedral surpassed Egypt's Great Pyramid, the Arab world has the tallest building.

"Downtown Dubai" is the flagship project of Emaar, a Dubai-based property developer that takes pride in making the impossible possible. The mixed-use mega-project is regarded as a beacon of progress, symbolizing the recently attained prosperity of the Middle East—specifically, that is, those parts of the region with only human ingenuity to draw on rather than energy resources.

Burj Khalifa, a vertical sky-city inspired by Frank Lloyd Wright's 1956 Mile High Illinois plan for Chicago, is, for the UAE, proof that Islam, globalization, and modernity can all coexist. Steel-ribbed and clad in aluminum and glass, 2,716-feet-tall Burj Khalifa has the equivalent of five Airbus A380s' worth of the metal. If laid end to end, the amount of rebar used (more than 31,000 metric tons) would have gone more than a quarter of the way round the world.

This embodiment of global superlatives—tallest building, tallest freestanding structure, highest observation deck, and more—is a stunning example of human can-do.

CATHEDRAL OF THE IMMACULATE CONCEPTION
CUENCA, EQUADOR

The Spanish viceroy founded the city of Santa Ana de los Cuatro Ríos de Cuenca in 1557, on the ruins of Tumibamba, the second city of the Inca empire.

At its greatest extent, Huayna Capac ruled the Inca empire mostly from his palace in this region, conquered from the Canari people in the 1480s. In 1530, when both he and his heir died from smallpox, a civil war divided the Inca just before Pizarro arrived in 1532. (*Cuenca* describes a river basin and the Spanish name derives from the valley's four rivers, one of which—Tumibamba—runs through the city.)

Cuenca was Cultural Capital of the Americas in 2002, and today, amid its cobblestoned streets and charming, colonial-era architecture, it is still possible to see how old palaces became the foundations for new structures. In the heart of the city, the oldest building (1557) is the Iglesia del Sagrario, the former cathedral built using stones from the ruined Inca city of Pumapungo nearby.

In 1885 work began on a new one, the Cathedral of the Immaculate Conception (right). It was completed in 1967 and it is said that the immense interior could then contain most of the population. Its sky blue cupolas stand out across the city and it has stained glass windows with both Catholic and indigenous symbols, such as the sun and moon.

AMPHITHEATER
EL DJEM, TUNISIA

This amphitheater is the largest of its kind in North Africa and could hold 35,000 spectators. It once hosted gory spectacles with wild animals, but today it is a setting for classical music concerts.

Although modern El Djem is unremarkable, as the Roman town of Thysdrus this was a wealthy center of olive oil production in the early centuries CE with many fine villas.

The amphitheater was begun in the 230s by Gordian, who was involved in an uprising in 238 against Emperor Maximinus. Gordian was briefly made emperor at Thysdrus before his forces were defeated within days. Later the same year his grandson became Gordian III (reigned 238–244), and further work on the amphitheater may have been to recognize the town's loyalty to the Gordian cause.

In the 1690s Ottoman forces blew down a wall while flushing out dissenters; however, the chambers beneath the arena remain well preserved. The basement gallery and lift shafts are exposed, and the underground passageways and areas where wild creatures were kept can be visited. Mosaics from local villas suggest particular interest in bloody entertainment that involved animals. It is even rumored that a transportation tunnel exists somewhere under the amphitheater that once led to the coast, more than 100 miles away.

SYDNEY OPERA HOUSE
NEW SOUTH WALES,
AUSTRALIA

In harmony with its exposed waterfront setting and the adjacent Sydney Harbour Bridge, the curvaceous "sails" of the Sydney Opera House's massive roof vaults have created one of the most shapely arts buildings in the world.

Containing seven primary venues, in 2011 this center attracted more than 1,300,000 people to 1,795 performances. In addition, about eight million tourists visited, with 300,000 taking guided tours. This radical structure is now the icon of Australia, but the journey there was fraught.

When Danish architect Jørn Utzon won the open competition in 1957, his new architectural form had only a basic design. During the building of the granite-clad podium and the distinctive vaulted shells, the project turned into a testing ground, requiring structural engineers Ove Arup & Partners. Even the special glazed tiles—more than a million of them—took years to develop. As controversy grew, Utzon was forced out in 1966.

In 1999 Utzon, with his son Jan, was re-engaged as a consultant to maintain the building's architectural integrity into the future. The reception hall was turned into a light-filled space and renamed the Utzon Room in 2004, and in 2006 a solid wall was inset with glass openings to provide the foyer with a harbor view.

In 2009 Jørn Utzon died aged 90, his work having joined the World Heritage List (2007) in his lifetime.

TERRACOTTA ARMY
XI'AN, CHINA

In 1974 farmers digging a well found fragments of statues. They had unearthed an army for the afterlife placed there 2,000 years earlier to protect the first ruler of the Qin dynasty—the man who reunified China, the First Emperor Shi Huangdi (reigned 221–210BCE)—in death.

During the next few years a series of pits were revealed in a giant mausoleum that covers an area of about 22 square miles. Three main pits are now enclosed in a museum site that is a major attraction, with about 8,000 lifesize model terracotta soldiers, horses, and bronze chariots.

The figures were mass-produced using molded parts (torso, limbs, head), but each was then given individualized features and details of uniforms and armor were sculpted. Once fired, painted, and equipped with bronze weaponry, the men were arranged in battle formation, in readiness to be animated in the afterlife.

There are also officials, acrobats, strongmen, animals, and musicians—an entire courtly retinue.

The emperor's tomb, less than a mile away, lies under a forested burial mound. Some 2,000 years ago, the historian Sima Qian wrote that it contained a world of wonders, with mountains of gold, stars of pearls and jewels, and rivers of quicksilver. The tomb is unexcavated—and soil analyses confirm high levels of mercury. Who know what awaits.

MOUNT RUSHMORE
SOUTH DAKOTA, USA

Blasted by dynamite out of the granite face of a mountain from 1927 to 1941, sculptor Gutzon Borglum's titanic carving represents the first 150 years of the USA's history through four pivotal presidents.

Borglum was a well-known showman in stone. In 1924 South Dakota's state historian Doane Robinson asked him to craft a giant group of figures from the American West as a tourist attraction. After selecting Mount Rushmore and its sunny eastern aspect, Borglum decided on something he felt was more nationally inspiring. The presidents symbolize phases of the USA's growth: Washington for the USA's creation; Jefferson for its expansion, doubling with the Louisiana Purchase in 1803; Lincoln, for the preservation of the nation's unity; and Roosevelt, for overseeing the country's development into a world power.

Immortalized in Alfred Hitchcock's 1959 thriller *North by Northwest*, the giant faces were cleaned for the first time in the mid-2000s, making it easier to spot the dark, broken drill-bit within Washington's left eyelid.

The site attracts several million visitors each year. In 2010 a 3-D laser scan was made of the mountain, in case the sculptures ever need to be re-created. The data will also help the National Park Service to create holographs for the classroom or to enable virtual visits and climbs of the monument to be made.

SUKHOTHAI HISTORICAL PARK
SUKHOTHAI, THAILAND

Between about 1240 and 1438 Sukhothai ("Rising of Happiness") flourished independently under rulers who had declared the state religion to be Theravada Buddhism.

The ruins of a golden age of Thai civilization now lie in Sukhothai Historical Park. The temple complexes make good use of ponds in their settings and are aligned east–west to the movement of the sun, with the spiritual and ceremonial focus being Wat Mahathat ("Great Relic Temple," right).

As well as Mon, Khmer, and Sri Lankan influences, there are also purely Thai forms. A type of *stupa* (*chedi*) was developed with a "lotus bud" profile. Whereas the posture of the Buddha is normally standing, sitting, or lying down, at Sukhothai he is also shown walking, with his right hand in the reassurance gesture— although the most common is his calling the earth to witness his enlightenment. Thai statuary is defined by its smooth clothing and the curved lines of the mouth and eyebrows, which continue into the long fine nose, above a gentle smile. The hair often peaks with a flame-like "wisdom bump" emerging from the top of the head (following pages).

The park is perfect for the Loi Krathong festival, held on the full moon at the end of the Thai lunar year when people put candles in floats on the water and the ruins are illuminated.

ANCIENT CITY OF SIGIRIYA
SIGIRIYA, SRI LANKA

The foundations are all that remain of this royal fortress atop a lofty outcrop of hardened magma, more than 600 feet tall, which dominates the verdant terrain for miles around.

Buddhist monks first carved out grottoes in this volcanic rock in the third century BCE. Their monastic retreat became a royal redoubt in the late fifth century CE when King Kassapa (reigned 477–495), having usurped the throne of his half-brother Moggallana, established his capital here. When Moggallana later returned with an army, Kassapa committed suicide.

At ground level the rock was surrounded by a wall, a moat, and a network of landscaped gardens. Sigiriya means "Lion's Rock" and the platform where the entranceway to the summit complex is located once consisted of a huge brick lion with a stairway between its paws and leading into its mouth. The paws and some of the steps of this Lion Gate can still be seen today.

The city is famous for its few remaining frescoes of graceful female figures and the so-called "mirror wall" of polished limestone, which is etched with verses and graffiti dating back to the sixth century.

Moggallana returned Sigiriya to the monks and a monastic complex remained here for centuries before it fell into decay. The site was rediscovered in the mid-1890s by British archaeologist, H.C.P. Bell.

WINTER PALACE
ST. PETERSBURG, RUSSIA

This grand palace on the bank of the Neva River in St. Petersburg was the official residence of the czars until February 1917 and today, as the Hermitage Museum, it is a major tourist attraction.

A reflection of the historic might of Russia, the vast palace has 1,500 rooms, 117 staircases, 1,786 doors, and 1,945 windows. The main north and south frontages—820 feet long—face the Neva and the city, respectively.

It was built in 1754–1762 for Empress Elizabeth Petrovna, a daughter of Peter the Great, and she died before it was completed. By 1764 Empress Catherine II (the Great) lived there. She bought 255 paintings for herself from a dealer in Berlin, which laid the foundation for today's museum. By 1783 the empress had 2,658 works of art—the largest collection in Europe.

The palace has had an incident-filled history. In 1837 a terrible fire meant it had to be rebuilt. In 1917 it was stormed by revolutionary mobs. In 1941, when the then city of Leningrad was besieged for 900 days, the staff had to transfer more than a million objects to Sverdlovsk (Yekaterinburg) for safekeeping.

In its modern guise as the largest museum and art gallery in Russia, it has been calculated that if you were to spend a minute with each exhibit—there are 2.7 million items—the visit would last for more than five years.

TEOTIHUACÁN
MEXICO

Ancient Mexico's first great metropolis was built early in the Common Era and had as many as 200,000 inhabitants, yet by the ninth century it had been abandoned.

It is not known what this once great ceremonial center was called, who built it, or why it collapsed. The Aztecs, who found it in the 1100s, named it Teotihuacán ("Birthplace of the Gods") and made it the setting for an important myth about two Aztec gods who sacrificed themselves to become the sun and moon and bring the present world, the Fifth Creation, into being.

The city's two major monuments are known today as the Pyramid of the Sun and the Pyramid of the Moon (right). Each site has mass graves of sacrificial victims. From the Pyramid of the Moon a broad thoroughfare called the Avenue of the Dead runs south for nearly two miles. This immense way ends at a sunken plaza known as the Ciudadela where there is a major temple adorned with imagery of a feathered serpent, which the Aztecs later inherited as Quetzalcoatl.

The monumental complex has become a modern-day center of pilgrimage. Up to a million people flock to the city's cosmically aligned structures each March for the spring equinox. Many climb the steps to the top of the Pyramid of the Sun to greet the rising sun—perhaps just as the city's builders did nearly two millennia years ago.

LASCAUX CAVE
MONTIGNAC, FRANCE

Ancient rock art and paintings provide us with some of the most powerful examples of humankind's attempts to relate to the universe.

In 1940 four small boys in southwest France chanced upon a complex of caves in the bedrock at Lascaux. Some call the site "the Sistine of the Stone Age" because its chambers contain 16,000-year-old art of 2,000 figures. (The cave art at Chauvet, featured in Werner Herzog's 2010 movie *Caves of Forgotten Dreams*, may well be the oldest, at 30,000 years.)

At Lasceaux the paintings were perhaps created to link man with the animal world in some magical way. One of the most dramatic places is an area known as the Rotunda or Hall of the Bulls, with white calcite walls covered with paintings—in red, brown, and yellow mineral pigments with outlines of black—of aurochs (an extinct bovine), horses, and other animals. These aurochs (right) on the north wall form part of a continous painting. One bull is about 17 feet long.

As if to emphasize a connection with the natural world, many of the images use the undulations of the rock to create the design.

The public is no longer able to enter the caves because of damage being caused by fungal growth. However, nearby is Lascaux II, a painstakingly detailed replica of the two main halls (including the Bulls) that is limited to 2,000 visitors a day.

PIAZZA DEL CAMPO
SIENA, ITALY

This asymmetrical, fan-shaped public space, dating from the late 1100s and known locally as il Campo ("the Field"), has been the principal setting for the Tuscan city's outpourings of communal pride and rivalry for 900 years.

The city's main marketplace once stood here because it did not belong to a *contrada*, the historical districts into which Siena is divided. Originally large enough to contain the entire population, this was the setting for public events, such as festivals, animal races, and executions.

In an era when some of Europe's cities were acquiring civic buildings to rival religious ones, the Republic of Siena's Council of Nine ruled from the town hall known as the Palazzo Pubblico (1288–1310) and its adjacent campanile, the Torre del Mangia (1338–1348). They were equal in height to the city's cathedral and represented parity between secular and Church power. These structures still dominate the piazza, where the ninefold pattern of the brick paving, dating to 1349, symbolizes the heritage of government by the Nine.

Twice a year, in July and August, thousands pack il Campo when it is turned into a racetrack for the

HUNGARIAN PARLIAMENT BUILDING
BUDAPEST, HUNGARY

The *Országház* ("House of the Nation") is the seat of Hungary's National Assembly and when it was built, between 1885 and 1904 on the east bank of the Danube, it was the largest parliamentary building in the world.

In 1880 the Diet approved a parliament to be located in the unified (1873) city of Budapest (Buda, Pest, and Óbuda). Imre Steindl's winning design was to be built on the flat plain of his native Pest, where it would dominate the view from Buda and its royal castle and palaces (right) in the old aristocratic capital.

Work on Steindl's vision began in 1885—an eclectic mix of styles, with a Gothic Revival exterior (inspired by London's Houses of Parliament) and an interior that has Baroque, Renaissance, and Byzantine elements. There are nearly 250 statues of Hungarian historical figures and coats of arms.

The building's height of 96 metres (315 feet) echoes the dates 896 (the establishment of the Principality of Hungary) and 1896, when the new parliament was inaugurated. Since 2000 the coronation crown of St. Stephen has been on show in the 16-sided domed hall at its center.

The patriotic poet Mihály Vörösmarty once lamented: "The nation lacks a home." Thanks to Steindl that is no longer true—sadly, he went blind before his great work could be seen, and in 1905 he died.

AL AIN OASIS
AL AIN, UNITED ARAB
EMIRATES

The city of Al Ain, on the traditional caravan route to Oman, has seven oases and has been a human settlement for some 4,000 years.

Al Jahili Fort (right), erected in the 1890s, was the birthplace in 1918 of the late Sheikh Zayed bin Sultan Al Nahyan, the founder of the United Arab Emirates (UAE). The fort was one of many built in the nineteenth and early twentieth centuries as bases from which the family could use its power to enforce peace between warring tribes, and to solidify Abu Dhabi's control of the palm grove oases prized by other Arab tribes, including those of Saudi Arabia. Al Ain, also called "the garden city," was verdant because of its traditional water distribution, known as the *falaj*, through underground channels, which have now largely fallen into disuse.

Al Jahili also served as a summer residence for the Al Nahyan family and until the slave trade was abolished by Sheikh Zayed in the 1960s it had been part of that ancient network of trade in human misery between sub-Saharan Africa and the Persian Gulf. The fort was restored in 2007–2008 and now houses a permanent exhibition of the work of British adventurer Sir Wilfred Thesiger (referred to locally with affection as "Mubarak bin London"), who visited in the 1940s during his crossings of the desert known as Rub' al Khali ("The Empty Quarter").

MONT SAINT-MICHEL
NORMANDY, FRANCE

For a millennium this tidal islet of faith was, along with Rome and Santiago de Compostela, one of the leading pilgrimage sites in the Western world—some say it is located astride a spiritual energy line.

The first church on the mount was consecrated in 709 and in 966 the Benedictines settled. The two main buildings today are the abbey church, with its Romanesque nave (1122–1135), and the "Merveille" (or "Marvel," 1203–1228), where the monks lived. A medieval town also developed.

During the Hundred Years' War the site was fortified with thick walls, which enabled the occupants to withstand a 30-year siege. Centuries later, during the revolutionary era, the abbey was closed and until 1863 it served as a prison. A religious community only returned to the site in 2001.

A daughter foundation exists at St. Michael's Mount in Cornwall, and French investigator Lucien Richer once speculated that a sacred alignment exists between various sites dedicated to St. Michael.

To protect the mount's status as a tidal islet—canals and polders have caused silt to build up in the bay—a special dam has been built and its effects should be felt within a few years, hopefully enabling the tide to come rushing in with fury and encircle the islet at great speed. Today, the pilgrims still come but more of the visitors are tourists—up to three million each year.

TIAN TAN BUDDHA
HONG KONG, CHINA

This monumental bronze Buddha was unveiled on the peak of Mount Muk Yue on Lantau Island in 1993. The statue symbolizes the newfound prosperity of China, the stability of Hong Kong, and peace on Earth.

The "Big Buddha" is 112 feet high and overlooks Hong Kong's largest Buddhist temple, Po Lin monastery. Its monks had been inspired in the 1970s during visits to Japan and Taiwan by the statues at Kamakura and Zhanghua. China's own tradition of monumental sculpture had declined over the centuries and the monks felt that to build a new one in Hong Kong would give people spiritual comfort. The template for the base platform came from Beijing's Altar of Heaven, which later gave the Buddha its name.

The design took its aesthetic form from Sui and Tang sculpture. Made out of 202 pieces of bronze mounted on a steel framework, the figure sits cross-legged on a lotus flower throne. Rather than facing south, as China's other statues do, it faces northeast—toward Beijing.

Once largely inaccessible, Mount Muk Yue is now one of Hong Kong's major attractions. On the hillside nearby is the Wisdom Path completed in 2002, which consists of a monumental calligraphic work: 38 tree trunks in a figure-of-eight configuration (for "infinity") and inscribed with characters that make up the 260-word *Heart Sutra*.

OCK HOUSES
APPADOCIA, TURKEY

This eerie and unearthly yet compellingly beautiful landscape owes its existence to historical acts of violence—geological, climatical, and human.

Millions of years ago a volcanic eruption left this plateau covered with layers of tuff, topped by basalt. Over eons of time this eroded into formations that geologists call hoodoos, some of which are 120-feet tall. People found the soft stone easy to work—and it hardens after exposure to the air.

Located between rival empires, the area was prone to marauders. Security came in the form of warrens of rooms and narrow passages, defended by rolled stone "gates"—difficult for any outsider to penetrate. Gradually, subterranean towns developed.

However, the most impressive structures are religious. Early Christian hermits and communities of monks created cells and chapels, and from the Byzantine period onward hundreds of churches were carved out, often brilliantly decorated inside. Uchisar (right), near Göreme Valley, is honeycombed with such places of worship as well as "troglodyte homes," cool storehouses for crops, and stables for animals.

This surreal scenery is a tourist attraction and it is popular to stay in a cave-hotel and float over the bizarre terrain in a hot air balloon. The greatest danger to this unique place remains the natural forces that made it all possible.

RED SQUARE
MOSCOW, RUSSIA

This open square has been popular with Muscovites for centuries. Its captivating sights make it easy for any visitor to appreciate why the square's name (*krasnaya*) originally translated as "beautiful."

The space has long been witness to Russia's history as the scene of public executions, riots, political dramas, state pomp, and parades—and, more recently, commercial events, from fashion to music. The east side is dominated by the department store GUM, opposite Lenin's tomb and the mighty walls and towers of the Kremlin, the forbidding center of temporal power.

However, most spirits soar at the spectacle of the Russian Orthodox St. Basil's (1555–1560, right) at the square's southern end. Eight chapels (dedicated to military victories) radiate from a main tower like an eight-pointed star. Commissioned by Ivan IV the Terrible, who named it (Cathedral of the Intercession) for the feast day on which his army captured Tartar Kazan in 1552, the church is popularly known after Vasily (Basil) the Blessed, whose grave lies beneath a chapel added in 1588.

The domes echo Islamic roofs (Byzantine ones were too vulnerable for the winter's snow) and dazzle today with their designs, but until the seventeenth and eighteenth centuries the domes were gold and the building was all white.

CLIFF PALACE
MESA VERDE, COLORADO, USA

The Anasazi people built this complex in the 1200s within an alcove overlooking Cliff Canyon, at an altitude of about 8,000 feet. It is the largest cliff dwelling in North America.

Cliff Palace has an area of about 260 feet by 65 feet and it is one of some 600 Native American cliff dwellings at Mesa Verde, which was made into a National Park in 1906 by President Roosevelt.

The Anasazi ("Ancient Ones") were hunter-gatherers who had moved to the mesa-tops to farm. In the 1150s they began to build in the cliff alcoves, but little more than a century later they had migrated further south, developing into today's Hopi and Zuni peoples.

Of the hundreds of Mesa Verde structures, 90 percent have ten rooms or fewer. Cliff Palace has 151 rooms, 23 *kivas* (the circular chambers dug into the ground and accessed from above by descending a ladder), and many open areas. There were probably 100–120 residents at Cliff Palace, with storage rooms for corn, beans, and squash.

With sandstone and timber beams to move, there must have been compelling reasons to build in these difficult locations—perhaps conflict or climate change. It may be significant that the *kivas* remain at the same temperature throughout the year, making them cool in summer and needing only a small fire to heat them in winter.

GRAND PLACE
BRUSSELS, BELGIUM

This imposing town square, the Grote Markt or Grand Place, is arguably the city's most memorable architectural landmark—an exuberant reminder of Flanders' mercantile past.

A public square surrounded by guild houses was once found in all Flemish towns. The ornate fronts on the gabled facades of the former private houses lend the space much of its appeal to the modern onlooker. A relatively uniform height gives cohesion, while swaggering individuality is provided by a profusion of decorative styles.

The contestation of the space is also interesting. Opposite the City Hall (1401–1455), the seat of municipal power, is the Duke of Brabant's so-called King's House or Breadhouse (on the old bread market, and rebuilt, right, in 1873), expressing the power of the nobility, which was then fading in the face of the rise of the local merchants and tradesmen. When the Grand Place was rebuilt after the devastating French bombardment of 1695, the guilds provided much of the energy and funds, and it is former guild houses (1690s–1700s) that now flank the Breadhouse. To the right is the artists' De Duif/Le Pigeon (numbers 26/27) where Victor Hugo lived when exiled in 1852.

Badly damaged by revolutionaries, most of the buildings were neglected until restoration efforts began in the late nineteenth century.

AÏT BENHADDOU
OUARZAZATE, MOROCCO

Much of the earthen architecture of Morocco reflects rural Berber influences. Crafted using compacted clay pisé, gravel, and sun-dried brick, it merges with the terrain from which it is derived—and returns to it if not maintained.

The best-known forms are the *ksar* and the *kasbah*. A *ksar* is a village built in a defensive mode, surrounded by its agricultural livelihood. A *kasbah*, probably derived from the Turkish word *kasabe* and meaning small town, has come to signify a fortified point in a city, but in southern Morocco and the High Atlas mountains a *kasbah* (*tighremt* in Berber) can be a vast fortress-village with spectacular tower houses, often decorated with checkerwork designs and geometric patterns.

The region of Ourzazate, at the confluence of three rivers and en route to the Sahara Desert, was once a stronghold of the powerful El Glaoui family, who ruled Marrakech and controlled the south from their many *kasbah*s in the area. Taourirt *kasbah* is the original part of the town of Ourzazate, which developed after the French Foreign Legion had allied with the El Glaouis during the French Protectorate and created an isolated outpost here in the 1920s. Well-preserved Aït Benhaddou (right) has provided the location for many films, including *Lawrence of Arabia*.

EILEAN DONAN CASTLE
KINTAIL, SCOTLAND

A postcard-perfect castle in the west of Scotland on the road to the Isle of Skye, Eilean Donan is nicknamed "the castle of dreams."

"The island of Donnán" is located at the point where three seawater lochs meet in the Gaelic-speaking Highlands. Miraculously, there is a freshwater well that enabled a Celtic Christian community to be established in the sixth century, but the first castle was not built until the thirteenth—to guard the territories of the Lordship of the Isles. That structure probably filled the entire site, but over time it decreased in size, probably because there was less need to muster manpower.

During the Jacobite Rebellion of 1715, several hundred Spaniards landed here and a gunpowder magazine was established at the castle to await the arrival of armaments from Spain, but they never came. British government forces then captured and destroyed the castle, which lay in ruins for two centuries until it was bought in 1911 by Colonel John MacRae-Gilstrap.

The mason Farquhar MacRae claimed to have had a dream in which every detail of how the castle once looked was revealed to him—and in 1920–1932 it was restored. Only later was the original ground plan discovered in the Edinburgh archives and, incredibly, found to match. Once the home of clan MacKenzie, it is now the home of their one-time protectors, clan MacRae.

PIC
TURE
CRE
DITS